Troubleshooting Citrix XenApp®

Identify and resolve key Citrix XenApp® issues using
trusted troubleshooting and monitoring techniques

Dragos Madarasan

Suraj Patil

BIRMINGHAM - MUMBAI

Troubleshooting Citrix XenApp®

First published: December 2015

Production reference: 1181215

Published by Packt Publishing Ltd.
Livery Place
35 Livery Street
Birmingham B3 2PB, UK.

ISBN 978-1-78528-378-9

www.packtpub.com

Credits

Authors
Dragos Madarasan

Suraj Patil

Reviewers
Mayur Arvind Makwana

Matthew M. Spencer

Commissioning Editor
Kartikey Pandey

Acquisition Editors
Shaon Basu

Prachi Bisht

Content Development Editor
Shali Deeraj

Technical Editor
Vivek Arora

Copy Editor
Merilyn Pereira

Project Coordinator
Sanchita Mandal

Proofreader
Safis Editing

Indexer
Tejal Daruwale Soni

Graphics
Kirk D'Penha

Production Coordinator
Melwyn Dsa

Cover Work
Melwyn Dsa

About the Authors

Dragos Madarasan works as a cloud support engineer for one of the largest IT companies in the world. After previous stints as a freelance IT consultant and working for a managed services provider, he now enjoys tackling complex scenarios and using his knowledge to help clients who have taken their business to the cloud.

Dragos publishes interesting cases on his personal blog and whenever time permits, he enjoys taking part in community-led events as a technical writer and speaker.

When not in front of a laptop, Dragos enjoys running and reading books on his Kindle.

Dragos has previously worked as a technical reviewer for *Microsoft SCCM High Availability and Performance Tuning* and *XenApp 6.5 Cookbook*, *Packt Publishing*.

Acknowledgments

I would like to thank my family for their long-time support and trust in me. I would never have been able to grow and learn as much as I did without your gracious support all these years.

I'd like to thank my closest friends, Ovidiu P, Calin D., and Radu E., who have been true friends, are always helpful, and never ask for anything in return.

I'd like to thank my former colleagues who supported and inspired me throughout my career—Tim Miltenberger, Calin Irimies, Sabin Georgescu, Mihai Breana, and everyone else I have worked with over the years.

A big thanks to the team responsible for publishing this book—my coauthor, *Suraj Patil*, who I have very much enjoyed working with. I would also like to thank our technical reviewers, Sebastiaan van Kaam and Matthew Spencer, who have kindly reviewed the book and made great suggestions.

I'd also like to thank Shaon Basu, our acquisition manager, who had the idea of putting this book together, and the team behind the book, Prachi Bisht, Shali Deeraj, and Ajinkya Paranjape, who have provided continuous feedback and helped edit this book.

Last but not least, I would like to thank the entire medical staff at the Nova Vita clinic who helped me recover after my accident.

Suraj Patil is an accomplished virtualization consultant with 8 years of experience in the information technology industry. He is a specialist in designing, building, maintaining, and optimizing Citrix, Microsoft, and VMware oriented infrastructures for large enterprises and mid-sized organizations. He holds a bachelor's degree in Information Technology and has many certifications from vendors such as Microsoft, VMware, Citrix, Red Hat, and Cisco.

Suraj is a Citrix Certified Professional — Mobility (CCP-M), VMware Certified Professional — Data Center Virtualization (VCP5-DCV), VMware Certified Professional — Network Virtualization (VCP6-NV), Microsoft Certified Solutions Expert (MCSE) — Private Cloud, and Cisco Certified Network Associate (CCNA).

Suraj currently lives in Mumbai and works for a Fortune 500 company as a Citrix consultant.

You can visit his blog at www.v12nsupport.com.

I would like to thank God for giving me the opportunity to write this book and share my knowledge with others.

I want to thank my family for the strength and the support they have always given me.

I want to thank Mr. Iqbal who gave me the opportunity to start working on the Citrix platform.

Special thanks to RK who pushed me to write and complete this book and always encouraged me to keep growing.

Finally, I would like to thank Deepti Thore, Shali Deeraj, Ajinkya Paranjape, Harshal Ved, and the entire staff at Packt Publishing for the support and patience during the writing of my first book.

Thank you all!!!

About the Reviewers

Mayur Arvind Makwana is a software IT specialist who holds a degree in computer engineering from India, and has more than 6 years of experience in the field of information technology, covering the Microsoft, Citrix, and VMware technologies. He is currently working on infrastructure operations for a Citrix (XenApp®/XenDesktop®) and Windows (WSUS/SCCM) project at one of the leading Fortune 500 companies. He is a huge believer in certification. His current certifications include the following:

- Citrix Certified Administrator for Citrix XenApp® 6.5 (CCA)
- Microsoft Certified Professional (MCP)
- Microsoft Specialist (Microsoft Server Virtualization with Windows Server Hyper-V and System Center)
- VMware Certified Associate – Data Center Virtualization (VCA-DCV)
- ITIL (Information Technology Infrastructure Library) V3 foundation
- ChangeBase AOK (Application Compatibility Testing and Remediation)
- Oracle Certified Associate (OCA)

Mayur writes technical blogs and helps troubleshooting issues for infrastructure operations at the Citrix Community as a volunteer. He has attended several courses and conducted training on topics such as the following:

- Licensing Windows Server
- Advanced Tools and Scripting with PowerShell 3.0 Jump Start
- Deploying Windows 8
- Licensing Windows 8
- Migrating from Windows XP to Windows 7
- Networking Fundamentals
- Introduction to Hyper-V Jump Start

He has also worked on the following books:

- *Microsoft Application Virtualization Cookbook, James Preston*
- *Windows PowerShell for .NET Developers, Chendrayan Venkatesan* and *Sherif Talaat*
- *Getting Started with PowerShell, Michael Shepard*
- *Troubleshooting Citrix XenDesktop®, Gurpinder Singh*

I would like to thank my mom, Beena Makwana, who has always encouraged me to utilize my potential and help people by sharing my expertise and knowledge. Thanks to the Packt Publishing team for giving me this opportunity.

Matthew M. Spencer is currently an architect, analyst, writer, and consultant. His career spans over 15 years across universities, state governments, software leaders, healthcare institutions, small businesses, and the Fortune 500. His work specializes in creating solutions to complex problems.

Matthew's projects have received many awards and accolades. Some of his proudest career achievements include an implementation of a multilingual collaboration and content management solution to 18,000 global users as well as creating a SaaS (Software as a Service) solution for a state government to sell technical services to other state governments for the purpose of interfacing with the FBI. Matthew has advanced to the second round of Verizon's Powerful Answers Award competition and was recently nominated to speak at TEDx. Matthew has also worked on the recently published *Microsoft Application Virtualization Cookbook*.

Matthew tweets often about technology at @chivalry and can be found at http://mattspencer.net/. He enjoys travelling the world, running endurance races, brewing his own beer, and contributing to The Good Judgment Project. He lives with his family in West Virginia.

I would like to thank my loving wife, Lisa Go, and my darling daughter, Isabella, for giving me their patience and time as I pursue my career goals and dreams. I would also like to thank my mentors, Bob and Connie Pirner, and Seth Roach, for all the countless advice along the way.

www.PacktPub.com

Support files, eBooks, discount offers, and more

For support files and downloads related to your book, please visit www.PacktPub.com.

Did you know that Packt offers eBook versions of every book published, with PDF and ePub files available? You can upgrade to the eBook version at www.PacktPub.com and as a print book customer, you are entitled to a discount on the eBook copy. Get in touch with us at service@packtpub.com for more details.

At www.PacktPub.com, you can also read a collection of free technical articles, sign up for a range of free newsletters and receive exclusive discounts and offers on Packt books and eBooks.

https://www2.packtpub.com/books/subscription/packtlib

Do you need instant solutions to your IT questions? PacktLib is Packt's online digital book library. Here, you can search, access, and read Packt's entire library of books.

Why subscribe?

- Fully searchable across every book published by Packt
- Copy and paste, print, and bookmark content
- On demand and accessible via a web browser

Free access for Packt account holders

If you have an account with Packt at www.PacktPub.com, you can use this to access PacktLib today and view 9 entirely free books. Simply use your login credentials for immediate access.

Instant updates on new Packt books

Get notified! Find out when new books are published by following @PacktEnterprise on Twitter or the *Packt Enterprise* Facebook page.

Table of Contents

Preface

In today's world, every organization has at least one or two applications that run their entire business.

Accessing these applications becomes mission-critical if the organizations want to sustain their businesses. Any users to get their job done need access to these critical applications.

Citrix XenApp with its FlexCast technology offers a flexible solution to mobilize Windows applications with a highly secure delivery model.

As with a large number of applications nowadays, XenApp requires minimal configuration and installation decisions and an experienced administrator can configure an infrastructure in a matter of minutes or hours. Particularly because installation is a simple process, it is troubleshooting that sometimes becomes difficult. Troubleshooting is not a science, it's an art form; and behind every issue there is a cause, so you must plan for the situation.

With this book, we will cover troubleshooting preparation, general processes, and real-world examples to resolve any XenApp issue in a proper manner.

By the end of this book, you will have enough knowledge to maintain and optimize your own Citrix XenApp environment.

What this book covers

Chapter 1, Basic Troubleshooting Methodology, covers understanding problems, breaking down problems into their affected components, and finally, testing problems.

Chapter 2, Understanding the Citrix® Components, introduces you to the supportive components that are part of the XenApp infrastructure. It will describe the process of starting a published application and how each component comes into play.

Chapter 3, Troubleshooting XenApp® Issues, explains standard troubleshooting processes and how to follow them to troubleshoot complex XenApp issues in a mission-critical environment.

Chapter 4, Troubleshooting Other Issues, covers troubleshooting with provisioning services, NetScaler Gateway, Citrix Storefront, and other infrastructure components.

Chapter 5, Monitoring and Optimizing, explains using Citrix Director, EdgeSight, and NetScaler Insight Center to optimize XenApp infrastructure.

What you need for this book

The following are the supported Windows operating systems:

- Microsoft Windows Server 2012 R2
- Microsoft Windows Server 2012
- Microsoft Windows Server 2008 R2 with Service Pack 1
- Microsoft Windows 8.1
- Microsoft Windows 8
- Microsoft Windows 7 with Service Pack 1

The following are the databases that can be used:

- SQL Server 2014, Express, Standard, and Enterprise Editions
- SQL Server 2012 SP1, Express, Standard, and Enterprise Editions
- SQL Server 2008 R2 SP2, Express, Standard, Enterprise, and Datacenter Editions

The following are the frameworks that can be used:

- Microsoft .NET Framework 4.5.1 (4.5.2 and 4.6 are also supported)
- Microsoft .NET Framework 3.5 SP1 (Windows Server 2008 R2 and Windows 7 only)
- Visual J# 2.0 SE
- Microsoft Visual C++ 2005, 2008, 2010, and 2013 Runtimes

You will also need one hypervisor such as Citrix XenServer, Microsoft Hyper-V, and VMware vSphere to create virtual machines.

Who this book is for

This book is for Citrix Administrators or Citrix Engineers, who are currently managing Citrix XenApp in the production environment and want to learn how to troubleshoot XenApp issues in the shortest time without missing a beat. It is assumed that readers have a basic understanding of XenApp components and how to implement and manage the XenApp infrastructure.

Conventions

In this book, you will find a number of text styles that distinguish between different kinds of information. Here are some examples of these styles and an explanation of their meaning.

Code words in text, database table names, folder names, filenames, file extensions, pathnames, dummy URLs, user input, and Twitter handles are shown as follows: "Delete the directory at C:\Program Files\Citrix\Receiver Storefront Directory."

A block of code is set as follows:

```
ODBC
\\ DRIVER= {SQL Native Client} \\ UID=administrator
\\ Trusted_Connection=Yes \\DATABASE =XA DS
\\ WSID=CTXXA02 \\ APP=Citrix IMA
\\ SERVER=CTXSQ02 \\ Failover_Partner=CTXSQ01
\\ Description=ds
```

Any command-line input or output is written as follows:

```
dsmaint config /user: ABCnetwork\administrator
/pwd:Passw0rd101 /dsn:"C:\Program Files
(x86)\Citrix\Independent Management Architecture\mf20.dsn"

DSMAINT RECREATELHC

RESTART IMASERVICE
```

New terms and **important words** are shown in bold. Words that you see on the screen, for example, in menus or dialog boxes, appear in the text like this: "Go to the virtual machine properties in **Virtual Device Node**, free up the position **0:0**."

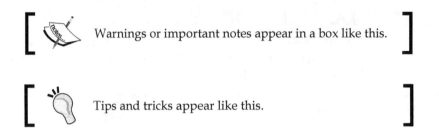

[Warnings or important notes appear in a box like this.]

[Tips and tricks appear like this.]

Reader feedback

Feedback from our readers is always welcome. Let us know what you think about this book—what you liked or disliked. Reader feedback is important for us as it helps us develop titles that you will really get the most out of.

To send us general feedback, simply e-mail feedback@packtpub.com, and mention the book's title in the subject of your message.

If there is a topic that you have expertise in and you are interested in either writing or contributing to a book, see our author guide at www.packtpub.com/authors.

Customer support

Now that you are the proud owner of a Packt book, we have a number of things to help you to get the most from your purchase.

Errata

Although we have taken every care to ensure the accuracy of our content, mistakes do happen. If you find a mistake in one of our books—maybe a mistake in the text or the code—we would be grateful if you could report this to us. By doing so, you can save other readers from frustration and help us improve subsequent versions of this book. If you find any errata, please report them by visiting http://www.packtpub.com/submit-errata, selecting your book, clicking on the **Errata Submission Form** link, and entering the details of your errata. Once your errata are verified, your submission will be accepted and the errata will be uploaded to our website or added to any list of existing errata under the Errata section of that title.

To view the previously submitted errata, go to https://www.packtpub.com/books/content/support and enter the name of the book in the search field. The required information will appear under the **Errata** section.

Piracy

Piracy of copyrighted material on the Internet is an ongoing problem across all media. At Packt, we take the protection of our copyright and licenses very seriously. If you come across any illegal copies of our works in any form on the Internet, please provide us with the location address or website name immediately so that we can pursue a remedy.

Please contact us at copyright@packtpub.com with a link to the suspected pirated material.

We appreciate your help in protecting our authors and our ability to bring you valuable content.

Questions

If you have a problem with any aspect of this book, you can contact us at questions@packtpub.com, and we will do our best to address the problem.

1
Basic Troubleshooting
Methodology

XenApp has grown into complex software with ever-expanding infrastructures in place. Together with tight integrations with other systems, such as Remote Desktop Services, Active Directory Domain Services, and other third-party authentication services, troubleshooting XenApp has become more complicated.

This first chapter will cover basic troubleshooting methodologies, how to approach troubleshooting complex issues, and what the full process entails—understanding the problem, finding a fix or workaround, determining the root cause, and applying corrective steps where applicable.

In this chapter, we will cover:

- Basic troubleshooting guidelines and methodologies
- Breaking down problems into affected components
- Resolution testing
- Root cause analysis and corrective actions

Troubleshooting 101

As with many software nowadays, XenApp requires minimal configuration and installation decisions, and an experienced administrator can configure the infrastructure in a matter of hours.

Particularly because the installation is a simple process, it is the troubleshooting that sometimes becomes difficult.

It is important to note that a solid grasp of XenApp components, interaction, and workflow is needed before performing troubleshooting.

Most times troubleshooting can be easy, either the solution is straightforward, perhaps because the administrator has experienced this problem in the past, or a simple Internet search for the particular error message will yield a Citrix knowledge-based article or blog post for that particular problem.

In all other cases, troubleshooting needs to be performed in an organized fashion so the solution is reached in the shortest amount of time possible, since many times the problem could involve downtime for a large number of users.

Although seemingly unimportant, one of the most important aspects of troubleshooting is producing a comprehensible problem statement:

- How is the problem manifesting itself?
- Who is facing the issue?
- When did the issue start?

Without clear answers to these questions, an ambiguous problem can undermine efforts for a solution.

Consider the fact that most of the time an issue is generally logged by a service desk or call center (first line of support), who might escalate it to a desktop support team (second line of support), and who will in turn escalate it to a *Citrix team* (third line of support).

If any piece of information is misunderstood by the analyst logging the incident, this in turn can be propagated to the Citrix team with the information being completely irrelevant to the troubleshooting process or even incorrect.

Consider the following scenario: a user working in the finance department calls the helpdesk and complains that an accounting application stopped working in Citrix. The application was working fine last week. The help desk agent performs a series of basic troubleshooting steps and escalates the problem to the next line of support without requesting additional information.

Consider the following questions:

- How many users are affected? Has the application stopped working for other users?
- What is the expected behavior of the application?
- Are you in the same location as last week or a new office?

- Is the application being used by a small or large number of users?
- Can the issue be reproduced on a different machine or in a different office?

While each question in itself might not directly lead to a solution, it can narrow down the problem considerably.

For instance, a positive answer to the first question might indicate this is a server or network issue as it affects multiple users.

A positive answer to the third question might indicate this is a network error; the next logical step would be to check whether there are any networking restrictions applied to subnets or IP addresses in the current location.

The fifth question is meant to check whether the issue is specific to a user, machine, or location.

Breaking down problems

When troubleshooting difficult cases, after making sure you have understood the problem (and that the information provided is correct and relevant), you must ensure a systematic approach to problem solving.

One strategy that can be used is *divide and conquer*, where you break down a problem into individual, easily solvable problems.

Considering the previous example where a user calls the helpdesk, one way of breaking down the problem is testing each *sub-system* individually, for example:

- Are the Citrix servers online and healthy? Check the monitoring systems.
- Is the network link reliable? Run a continuous ping and check whether websites load correctly.
- Is the problem easy to reproduce on any machine or does the problem *follow* the user?

For instance, in the case of XenApp 7.5/7.6, the following components can be considered:

- Server/desktop operating system machines and virtual delivery agents
- Delivery controller
- StoreFront
- Citrix receiver
- NetScaler Gateway

Going back to our example, one or more components can be causing a problem. For instance, there might be a problem with the **Virtual Delivery Agent (VDA)** on the server/servers hosting the finance application. This prevents the controller from being able to use the broker agent part of the VDA to communicate with the server.

Another possibility is that the issue is related to authentication. The StoreFront or the NetScaler Gateway (if the user is outside the corporate network) might have problems authenticating users to site resources.

It is important to quickly rule out as many components as possible. For instance, we could quickly test if the Citrix web page is accessible internally (where only the StoreFront component is used) and externally (where we might be reaching a NetScaler Gateway first). If the webpage is accessible internally but not externally, we would need to focus our attention on the NetScaler Gateway.

Alternatively, if, in both scenarios, the webpage does not load, we might focus our attention on the actual servers and/or delivery controllers.

Let's take another example: several users complain that during the day, applications published in XenApp start to become slow every morning.

The users mention that the slowness has been happening for some time, but it has only started to impact them recently.

Consider the following questions:

- How long has the initial slowness been observed (several weeks or months)?
- Around what hour is the impact noticeable?
- How long is the impact — several hours or the entire day?
- How often does the problem occur — on a daily basis or only on specific days?

Answers to the these questions can be tremendously important when dealing with performance-related issues. For example, it is important to establish whether the performance is affected during specific hours/days (to help to isolate whether a scheduled operation is causing the issue) and whether it is consistent (for example, happens every day of the week or happens only on specific dates/days).

Further breaking down the problem could consist of:

- Determining whether there is any correlation between systems tasks (antivirus, backup, web filtering, and so on) and the start of the slowness
- Determining whether the impacted application(s) can be tied to a group of servers, users, or user locations
- Analyzing past monitoring data for any negative performance trends

Use NetScaler Insight Center to collect information about traffic, performance data, and session information for NetScaler Gateway.

Resolution testing

Before describing how resolution testing should be done by administrators when troubleshooting a XenApp environment, there are two terms that need explaining. In software development terms, **resolution testing** is known as the process of retesting a bug once the development team has released a fix.

Regression testing is another methodology where test cases are re-executed for previously successful test cases.

Both testing methods are an important part of testing a software solution, as sometimes fixing one bug can cause regressions in other parts of the solution leading to new bugs.

Citrix administrators need to think in the same manner as testers do. Once the problem has been understood and a fix has been identified, then the fix or workaround can be applied. Once the fix is applied, the next step is to attempt to reproduce the initial issue. If this is not successful, it would generally mean the initial issue is resolved and most of the time that is the case.

However, besides testing for the initial issue, a Citrix administrator should also perform a number of tests to ensure that the fix does not negatively affect the XenApp infrastructure in another manner, for example, another application might stop working.

Root cause analysis

Once the problem has been correctly understood, and a fix applied and tested, the next step would be to determine the root cause and apply corrective actions if needed.

The **Root Cause Analysis and Corrective Actions (RCCA)** is the final step in troubleshooting a problem and involves determining the root cause of the issue and outlining any suggestions and recommendations for actions that can be implemented to prevent the reoccurrence of the underlying issue.

Most of the problems encountered in the Citrix world can be grouped into three categories:

- Performance issues, for example, applications are slow to start, the network is unreliable, and so on
- Incorrect configuration, for example, XenApp is not properly configured during the initial installation or a subsequent change
- Broken code leading to unexpected behavior from XenApp or underlying components — these are trickiest to debug and probably the least encountered

Most root cause analysis reveal either a performance issue or an incorrect configuration.

Where a root cause is deemed to be performance related, tackling them usually requires improvements in the infrastructure — bigger bandwidth, more servers, faster disks, and so on. The real challenge is determining how much to scale the infrastructure so that performance falls back within acceptable parameters without spending a large amount of money.

Preventive steps for these types of problems could be:

- Ensuring a capacity management process is in place
- Monitoring Citrix infrastructure for active usage
- Creating an easily scalable Citrix architecture

Incorrect configurations are usually self-evident; for example, if an administrator performs a change that negatively affects the Citrix infrastructure, again usually almost immediately. The root cause analysis, therefore, focuses on the following questions:

- Has the change management process been followed?
- Have the risks been properly established and highlighted?
- Have actions been considered to minimize the risks?
- Is there a backup plan in place in case a rollback is needed?
- What is the impact of a failed change and how will it affect users or production environments?

Changes where the risks have been appropriately highlighted ("Changing X setting has the risk of bringing down the Citrix site for 15 minutes"), where the change is performed out of hours (minimizing risks) and has a proper rollback plan in place are perfectly acceptable.

Most changes have the potential of causing downtime, but if the proper change management process is followed, the risks are minimized and the potential outage reduced.

Preventive steps for this type of problems could be:

- Ensuring the risks have been correctly identified and presented to the business
- Ensuring steps to minimize the risks have been identified
- Ensuring there is a clear backup plan in place

Finally, during troubleshooting, a number of changes might need to be done before the final fix is found. It is, therefore, a good idea to keep a track of these changes while the troubleshooting process is actively ongoing.

Once the correct fix has been identified, a retroactive change request should be logged in the IT system. Although, in this instance, the change hasn't followed the standard change management approval process, it is still useful to have changes logged in the system in case they need to be looked up in the future as part of troubleshooting previous changes.

Summary

In this chapter, we covered the basic methodologies of troubleshooting. We've described troubleshooting as first understanding the problem, breaking down the problem into its affected components, and finally, testing. The problems are solved once the fix or workaround is identified.

We highlighted the fact that sometimes, problems can be traced back to scheduled changes in the infrastructure, and that keeping track of changes is important as it can help in identifying the problem and mitigating or resolving it.

Finally, we discussed the root cause analysis, the process of determining the root cause of the issue (not just the fix/workaround) and preventive steps to minimize the reoccurrence of the issue.

In the next chapter, we will cover the Citrix XenApp/XenDesktop components, identifying and describing each one briefly. We will then talk about how the components interact and which communication channels are used during the interaction.

2
Understanding the Citrix® Components

In this chapter, you will understand the individual components and interactions required for a successful XenApp environment, which will aid in troubleshooting and finding the source of issues.

The following topics will be covered in this chapter:

- Identifying components and roles
- Understanding components and how they interact
- Communication channels

Identifying components and roles

As of XenApp 7.5/7.6, there are several components we need to take into consideration when troubleshooting issues. Citrix administrators who have worked with previous versions of XenApp will find that some of the components have changed significantly after XenApp was moved to the **FlexCast Management Architecture (FMA)**. With the older **Independent Management Architecture (IMA)** being dropped in favor of FlexCast, some of the core concepts have changed; farms are now called delivery sites, delivery controllers have replaced zone and data collectors, and worker groups have been replaced by session machine catalogs and delivery groups. The Citrix data store, which previously would use Microsoft Access database, is now a proper Microsoft SQL Server database.

We will discuss the following components of a XenApp site:

- Database
- Delivery controller
- License server
- Studio
- Virtual delivery agent
- Hypervisor
- StoreFront
- Receiver
- NetScaler Gateway

The database component

A major rewrite of the database component was performed as part of the switch to the FlexCast Management Architecture. Should the database become unresponsive, existing user sessions are maintained; however, no new connections will be possible.

The new feature called connection leasing was introduced by Citrix in XenApp 7.6. It allows users to connect and reconnect to applications used in the past (the default is 2 weeks and is configurable) even if the database server is down. This works by allowing the delivery controller to cache user connections and allows them to be replayed to the StoreFront in case the database is down.

Although these features allow users to continue working while the site database is down, Citrix recommends implementing fault tolerance by using SQL mirroring, clustering, or SQL AlwaysOn availability groups.

Further information can be found at `http://support.citrix.com/proddocs/topic/xenapp-xendesktop-76/xad-connection-leasing.html`.

When implementing XenApp, it is also important to use a Microsoft SQL Server version that is actively supported by Citrix to prevent potential compatibility or performance issues. This is especially important if a support case is opened with Citrix.

Citrix maintains a list of supported databases at `http://support.citrix.com/article/CTX114501`.

Information regarding high availability can be found at `http://support.citrix.com/proddocs/topic/xenapp-xendesktop-76/xad-plan-high-availability.html`.

The delivery controller

The delivery controller is likely the most vital part of XenApp since it is responsible for brokering by distributing desktops and applications and also manages the user access.

The delivery controller sits in the middle of the infrastructure and communicates with the site database, the virtual delivery agents installed on physical or virtual machines, StoreFront (or web interface), and also with Citrix Studio and Director.

Additionally, the delivery controller communicates with the underlying hypervisors for tasks such as machine creation and provisioning, administration, and others.

The delivery controller relies on a number of services to function, with the most important being:

- **Broker service**: As the name suggests, the broker service is responsible for creating new sessions but is also used during the resource enumeration phase and when the secure ticket authority is used

- **Machine creation services and host service**: These are used by XenDesktop to talk to the underlying virtual infrastructure (XenServer, VMware, and Hyper-V) during virtual machine provisioning

- **AD identity service**: This is used by XenDesktop to manage active directory computer accounts

- **Configuration Logging service**: This is used to log administrator activity and can be very useful when performing troubleshooting or for compliance

- **Configuration service**: This stores the configuration of the Citrix service

- **StoreFront service**: This is used to manage the StoreFront deployment

- **Monitor service**: This is used to monitor the **FlexCast Management Architecture (FMA)**

- **Delegated Administration service**: This is used to manage and configure delegated administration permissions

In XenApp 7.6, all delivery controllers are regarded as active-active, and as such, should a delivery controller go offline, others will be used by users. This approach is different in the previous versions of XenApp. In XenApp 6.5 and previous versions, one server would get elected as a zone data collector and be responsible for orchestration. In the event the server goes down, the other servers would elect another zone data collector among themselves. This process is now obsolete in versions 7.5 and later where all delivery controllers are considered active.

The license server

Every XenApp infrastructure has at least one license server and Citrix does not recommend deploying more than one server.

The license server is usually never a single point of failure as XenApp farms will continue running for 30 days even if the license server is down, but there are a few instances when troubleshooting the licensing server can become important. Migrating from major versions of XenApp sometimes causes issues with the licensing server, which we will discuss in a further chapter.

Studio

The XenApp Studio is the main console used for administration and is used by both XenApp and XenDesktop. StoreFront can be partly administrated from the Studio console as well but comes with its own management console.

The XenApp Studio console can be used to manage both on-premises and cloud infrastructures.

The Virtual Delivery Agent (VDA)

The **Virtual Delivery Agent** (**VDA**) is a component installed on any server (physical or virtual, desktop or server OS) and manages the session connection between the user and published resources.

The delivery controller listens for the virtual delivery agents to register with the controller. The VDA is also responsible for handling ICA/HDX connections and applying session policies to virtual desktops.

Hypervisor

XenDesktop provides two provisioning mechanisms—**Machine Creation Services** (**MCS**) and **Provisioning Services** (**PVS**).

As part of Machine creation services, XenDesktop supports XenServer, VMware ESX, and Microsoft Hyper-V.

At the time of writing, the following virtualization platforms are supported:

- XenServer 6.1, 6.2 SP1, and 6.5
- VMware vSphere 5 and later
- Hyper-V

- Amazon Web Services
- Citrix CloudPlatform

 Citrix technical support has engineers with experience in troubleshooting the preceding virtualization solutions; however, they can only provide limited assistance when dealing with unsupported versions of these virtualization platforms.

See `http://support.citrix.com/article/CTX131239` for an updated list of supported platforms.

When used in combination with XenServer, XenApp communicates using the XenServer Management API commonly referred to as XenAPI. XenAPI is an open source software and uses an XML-RPC based format allowing programmatic access to XenServer.

Read more about the XenServer 6.5.0 Management API Guide at `http://support.citrix.com/article/CTX141506`.

If used with VMware's ESXi, XenDesktop/XenApp requires VMware vSphere 5 or later and uses the VMware vSphere Web Services SDK for integration and communicates on port 80/443.

Machine Creation Services integrates with Hyper-V by leveraging System Center Virtual Machine Manager 2012 or later.

StoreFront™

Citrix StoreFront is the successor to web interface with Citrix recommending all new deployments to be designed around StoreFront, although web interface is still supported until August 2016.

Citrix StoreFront is an enterprise application store that allows the IT department to provide personalized applications and desktops to users across multiple sites and farms. StoreFront simplifies management and benefits from the latest improvements in enterprise security while allowing administrators to maintain and enforce their security policies.

The StoreFront is one of the two authentication solutions that can be used with XenApp/XenDesktop. The StoreFront talks to both the delivery controller and the Receiver.

The StoreFront is responsible for enumerating the applications or desktops published for a user by communicating with the delivery controller.

StoreFront allows users to mark applications as favorites and is also responsible for generating the launch file (the `.ica` extension).

StoreFront communicates with the Delivery controllers on ports 80 and 443 and queries the SQL Server database (port 1433) for user subscription information.

For very large infrastructures, a special consideration needs to be taken: all the StoreFront servers in a group must reside within the same domain as per the Citrix design document (`http://support.citrix.com/proddocs/topic/dws-storefront-25/dws-plan.html`).

Receiver™

Citrix Receiver is the component installed on the user device. The receiver will communicate either directly or indirectly with the StoreFront or NetScaler servers and with servers running the virtual delivery agents.

A distinct component called Receiver for HTML5 provides access to desktops and applications in the same manner as Citrix Receiver but does not require a client-side installation. Instead, it uses the StoreFront API together with an HTML5 capable browser to achieve the same effect.

A receiver for HTML5 is supported on the latest versions of the major browsers: Internet Explorer (IE10 and IE11), Safari (6 and 7), Google Chrome (36 or later), and Mozilla Firefox (31 or later). Additionally, Receiver for HTML5 requires StoreFront version 2.5 or later and will not work with web interface.

Citrix Receiver communicates with the StoreFront component and alternatively with the NetScaler Gateway on ports 80/443.

In addition, there are a number of thin clients that come with Citrix Receiver preinstalled.

Learn more and browse Citrix-compatible products at `https://citrixready.citrix.com/`.

NetScaler Gateway™

The NetScaler Gateway is the solution provided by Citrix for secure external access. Initially developed by NetScaler, a company which Citrix later acquired, NetScaler Gateway has replaced Citrix Secure Gateway as the recommended method of securing external access.

NetScaler Gateway comes either as a hardware appliance (NetScaler Gateway MPX and NetScaler Gateway 9010 FIPS editions) or a software appliance NetScaler Gateway VPX. Depending on the number of remote users that the NetScaler Gateway needs to cater to, you would choose either the software or hardware appliance.

As any kind of external access would require passing through the NetScaler Gateway, Citrix recommends deploying NetScaler Gateways in pairs of two, to provide for high availability and load balancing.

The NetScaler Gateway component interacts with a number of other components:

- Active Directory for authentication purposes (which uses port 389 or 636)
- Virtual delivery agent to grant access to applications and desktops (ICA/HDX protocols and ports 1494 and 2598)
- Delivery controllers to parse application and desktop requests (ports 80, 8080, and 443)

Component interaction

To understand how the different XenApp/XenDesktop components interact, it is important to first understand the XenDesktop **FlexCast Management Architecture (FMA)** and the easiest way to do this is to highlight the main steps taken when starting a published application or desktop.

The following steps assume XenDesktop 7.5/7.6 is used together with Citrix StoreFront and/or NetScaler Gateway. The scenario where web interface is used instead of StoreFront is not taken into account:

1. The user initiates the connection using Citrix Receiver or a browser; ports 80 or 443 are used for the communication. The connection is made to the StoreFront or to the NetScaler Gateway if the user is external.

   If the user is authenticating against a NetScaler Gateway (an external user), then the NetScaler validates the user against Active Directory using port 389 and forwards the validated user credentials to the Citrix StoreFront on port 443.

2. StoreFront will authenticate the user by connecting to a domain controller on port 389.

   Once the user is successfully authenticated, StoreFront next checks the data store for any subscriptions by the user and subsequently stores them in memory.

3. StoreFront forwards the user credentials to the delivery controller using ports 80/443.

4. The delivery controller *validates* the credentials against Active Directory (port 389).

 Note there is a difference between user authentication, authenticating a user, and user validation, which is the process of determining the resources assigned to a user.

5. The XenApp delivery controller queries the SQL database for the available resources once the validation process has finished. By default, the SQL database listens on port 1433.

6. The delivery controller sends StoreFront information regarding the available resources. StoreFront populates the user's session with the available resources.

   In the case of an external user, the list of resources is passed through the NetScaler Gateway.

7. A user selects a published resource in the browser or Citrix Receiver. The request is sent to the StoreFront on port 80/443 and through the NetScaler Gateway in the case of a remote user.

8. StoreFront receives the request and forwards it to the delivery controller on port 80/443.

9. The delivery controller queries the SQL database to establish the host, which will carry out the request.

10. The delivery controller sends the connection information to StoreFront. StoreFront creates the .ica launch file and sends it to the user.

    In case of a remote user, StoreFront will contact a **Secure Ticket Authority (STA)** and request a ticket. The STA is hosted on the delivery controllers and will generate a unique ticket for the user, valid for 100 seconds.

    The information in the ticket contains the requested resource, server address, and port number.

    Similar to the previous steps, in case of a remote user, the launch file (containing the above ticket information) is sent to the user through the NetScaler Gateway.

11. Citrix Receiver opens the launch file and connects to the resource using ports 1494 or 2598.

    When a remote user launches the file, it connects to the NetScaler Gateway on port 443. The NetScaler Gateway will validate the ticket against the STA (delivery controller) on port 443.

    Finally, NetScaler Gateway initiates a connection on behalf of the user to the resource (port 1494/2598).

12. In any XenApp/XenDesktop implementation, there are two typical scenarios where it is important to understand the components being used and how they interact:

    ° XenApp/ XenDesktop for internal access

    ° XenApp/ XenDesktop for external access

XenApp®/XenDesktop® internal access scenario

This is the simplest scenario and assumes a user is attempting to start a published application in a XenApp 7.5/7.6 farm:

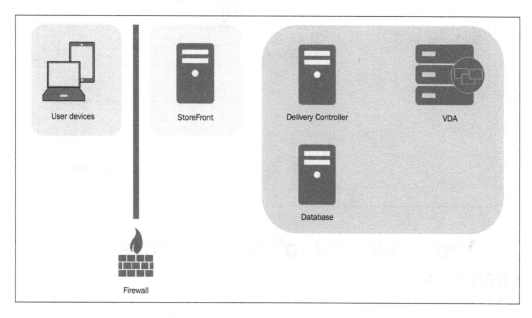

In this type of deployment, the following components are used: Citrix Receiver, StoreFront, XenApp delivery controllers, and virtual delivery agent.

The scenario and component interaction is exactly the same regardless of whether a user is accessing published applications or hosted desktops.

Internal access component interaction

In this scenario, the user device (either an HTML5 capable browser or Citrix Receiver) communicates with the StoreFront component on ports 80/443 and then directly with the virtual delivery agent once the launch file is opened.

StoreFront in turn communicates with the delivery controller(s) who query the Microsoft SQL database:

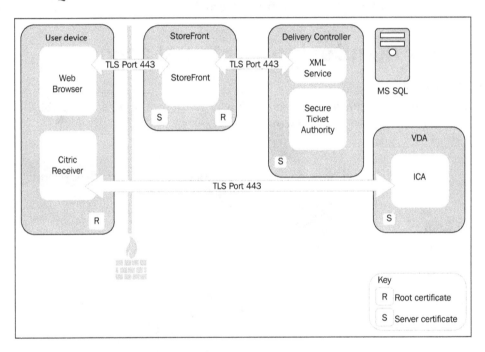

XenApp®/XenDesktop® remote access scenario

In the second scenario, the user is now external and will access the resources through a NetScaler Gateway, the components being used are otherwise the same:

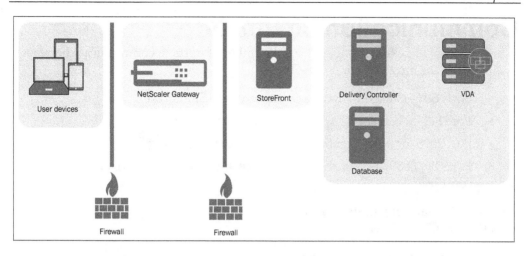

External access component interaction

In this scenario, the NetScaler Gateway is used to route all traffic between the client and the backend XenApp infrastructure. NetScaler Gateway will secure all traffic between the user devices and hosted desktops/applications using the **Transport Layer Security (TLS)** encryption protocol:

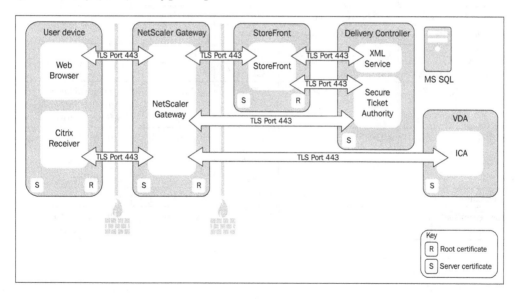

Communication channels

While XenDesktop/XenApp uses a large number of ports to communicate between components, the most common ones are:

- Ports 80/443 used by Receiver to connect to StoreFront
- Port 1494 when the ICA/HDX protocol starts
- Port 2598 for Session reliability (if enabled)
- Ports 80/8080/443 for the XML service and 2513 for the Citrix Management console

The following table illustrates the complete list of ports used by XenApp/XenDesktop 7.5 and later:

Source	Description	Type	Port (s)	Details
User (External) NS Gateway	Internal Network through	TCP	443	
User (Internal)	StoreFront	TCP	80/443	Connecting to the Store or Receiver for the website hosted on the StoreFront server.
Delivery Controller	Active Directory	TCP	389/636	
Delivery Controller	Microsoft SQL Server	TCP	1433	
Delivery Controller	Citrix License Server	TCP	2700/7279	
Delivery Controller	XenServer	TCP	80/443	
Delivery Controller	Microsoft SCVMM Server	TCP	8100	Communication with the Hyper-V infrastructure
Delivery Controller	VDA	TCP	80/443	The WorkstationAgent. exe process communicates with Controller
NetScaler Gateway	StoreFront	TCP	80/443	
NetScaler Gateway	LDAP Server	TCP/UDP	389/636	389: Used for the LDAP connection
(Active Directory				
Domain Controller)				636: Used for an LDAP SSL connection
NetScaler Gateway	Radius Server	TCP/UDP	1645/1812	RADIUS connection

Source	Description	Type	Port (s)	Details
NetScaler Gateway	VDA	TCP/ UDP	1494/2598	1494: Access to applications and desktops by means of standard ICA/HDX
				2598: Session Reliability enabled
NetScaler Gateway	Delivery Controller	TCP	80/8080/443	Application/Desktop request through XML service
NetScaler Gateway	Secure Ticket Authority	TCP	80/8080/443	STA embedded into XML service
Provisioning Services	Citrix License Server	TCP	27000/7279	27000: Handles initial point of contact for license requests (Lmadmin.exe)
				7279: Handles the check-in/check-out of licenses
Provisioning Services	Microsoft SQL Server	TCP	1433	
Provisioning Services	Domain Controller	TCP	389/636	Communication with Active Directory services
StoreFront	Domain Controller	TCP/ UPD	389/88/464	389: LDAP connection to query user-friendly names and e-mail address
StoreFront	Microsoft SQL Server			88: Native Windows authentication protocol to validate domain user credentials
StoreFront	StoreFront Server			464: Native Windows authentication protocol to allow users to change expired passwords
StoreFront	Delivery Controller	TCP	1433	Only StoreFront 1.2 and earlier. Used to connect StoreFront and SQL server to read/write application information to the subscription database.

Source	Description	Type	Port (s)	Details
VDA	Delivery Controller	TCP	Random	Only StoreFront 2.0 and later. Used for peer-to-peer services (credential wallet, subscriptions store). Service uses MS .Net NetPeerTcpBinding that negotiates random ports on each server between peers. Only used for communication within the cluster.
VDA	Provisioning Server	TCP	80/443	For application and desktop requests
XenApp	XenApp	TCP	3268	Communication between VDA and Microsoft Global Catalog used during the registration process.
XenApp	Microsoft SQL Server DNS	TCP	6910-6930	
XenServer	Service	TCP	2512	Worker to Controller and Controller to Controller communication
XenServer	Domain Controller	TCP	1433/1434	1434: Required for named instance connections; uses UDP
		TCP/ UDP	53	
		TCP	389/636	389: User authentication when using AD integration (LDAP) 636: LDAP over SSL (LDAPS)

A complete list of ports can be found on `http://support.citrix.com/article/ CTX101810`.

Summary

In this chapter, we identified the components that are part of the XenDesktop/XenApp infrastructure and briefly discussed the role of each component in a site deployment and how they interact with each other.

To better understand where each component is used, we described the process of starting a published application and how each component comes into play.

We discussed the two main scenarios — accessing resources in an internal network and accessing resources externally using NetScaler Gateway.

We mentioned the communication channels (protocols and ports) used by the main components such as Receiver, the ICA/HDX protocols, and we provided the full list of ports and protocols used by the XenDesktop/XenApp services.

In the next chapter, we will discuss specific issues around XenApp/XenDesktop and StoreFront and learn how to identify and resolve them.

3

Troubleshooting XenApp® Issues

In this chapter, we will see how to identify and troubleshoot the real life XenApp and its component-related issues.

We will cover the following topics in this chapter:

- Preparation for troubleshooting
- The troubleshooting processes
- Examples of common XenApp issues
- Troubleshooting tips for known issues

Preparation for troubleshooting

As troubleshooting is not a science, it's an art form, and behind every issue there is a cause so you must prepare a plan for the situation. Our action is most important whenever we start looking to resolve any technical issues.

Let's assume some user has reported a performance issue with a particular application that is published through Citrix XenApp 6.5. Now, in this situation, there will be two possibilities: one is that you are already aware of such issues (if it is, then you will get it solved quickly) and the second possibility is that it is the first time you are facing such an issue in your career.

Now, here you as a Citrix administrator start troubleshooting on a reported issue. But before starting troubleshooting on any new problem, we should follow some troubleshooting processes to get a quick resolution of the reported issue.

Troubleshooting processes

Let's have a look at the troubleshooting processes we should follow before starting XenApp troubleshooting:

- Gather proper information
- Identify the issue
- Try some quick fixes
- Use appropriate diagnostic steps
- Perform a quick search on the Internet
- Use additional resources to research the issue
- Escalate the issue if required

Gathering proper information

Once the user reports the issue, the Citrix administrator should gather appropriate information about the problem. While gathering information, we should consider the questions listed here. The following questions and their answers will make the troubleshooting task easier:

- What are the details of your Citrix XenApp environment?

  The version and edition of XenApp, farm size, type of data store, operating system, service packs, Hotfixes, network architecture, access gateway or NetScaler details.

- What is the exact issue?

  This specifies what is happening and what should happen.

- When did it start? What caused this issue?

  For example, this issue happened in a peak hour or all of sudden.

- What are the steps to reproduce this issue?

  Do you know the steps to reproduce the issue? If yes, then what are these steps? If not, why?

- Who is affected by this issue?

  A single user, a group of users, or all users including administrators.

- Which type of client is in use?

  Citrix Receiver or Online Plug-in version.

- Does this issue affect a single server or all servers?

  It might be a farm server issue, license server, or web interface server, for example.

- Do you get an error prompt or an event in the event log?

  The exact error messages or event log entries will make researching the problem easier.

- Can you reproduce this issue using an RDP session?

  You must try this out for better identification of any application and VDI related issues.

- What troubleshooting steps have you taken to reproduce the same issue?

  You must note what steps you have followed while troubleshooting these issues, as all this information will be required if escalating these issues to Citrix Technical Support teams.

> The Citrix Consulting team keeps us continuously updated on how to troubleshoot Citrix issues they have identified in their tech-support practices (http://support.citrix.com/pages/troubleshooting/). Here, we will find multiple troubleshooting guides and technotes published by Citrix Support teams.

Identifying the issue

For every technical problem, we have to select the appropriate action to identify it and investigate thoroughly the indications of that problem and its possible location.

Sometimes, the error message itself can give us a clear indication of where exactly the problem occurred and its root cause.

Let's see the following example illustrating errors encountered while installing XenApp components:

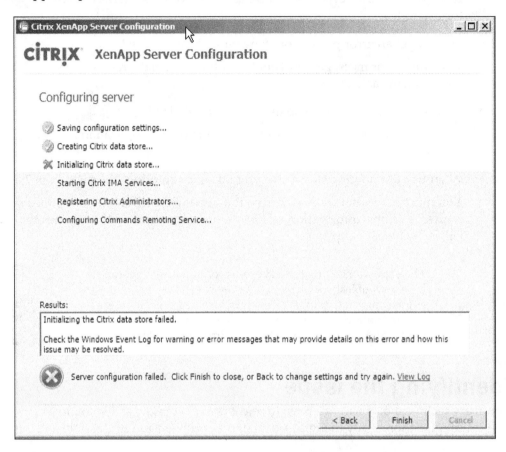

In the preceding error screenshot, the error reads **Initializing the Citrix data store failed**.

It clearly indicates that we should have a look at the farm name, database name, or authentication for the appropriate SQL instance.

 Sometimes, in similar scenarios, preinstalled Hotfixes might cause other issues.

Trying some quick fixes

Ok, we have identified the issue. Now what next? Is there any tool available for quick fixes for small issues?

Yes, there is…. Let's have a look at some Citrix tools that can be used for quick fixes:

- **Citrix Scout**: This can be run from a Citrix XenApp server to capture traces and data of selected end user systems. It can securely upload to Citrix TaaS servers to allow the Citrix Technical Support team to troubleshoot if needed. Citrix Scout is available at `http://support.citrix.com/article/CTX130147`.

- **XDPing Tool**: This is commonly known as the XenDesktop Ping tool, it can be used to check the configuration issues in a XenDesktop environment. XDPing tool is available at `http://support.citrix.com/article/CTX123278`.

- **Print Detective**: This is a utility to collect printer-related information for troubleshooting print driver issues. We can use this tool to delete specified print drivers on the XenApp server. Print Detective is available at `http://support.citrix.com/article/CTX116474`.

- **HDX Monitor**: This is a tool to identify, diagnose, and monitor Citrix HDX components. The HDX Monitor tool is available at `http://support.citrix.com/article/CTX135817`.

- **MedEvac 2.5**: This can be used to check the following components of a Citrix XenApp farm:
  - XML Service health
  - Verify the data collector health
  - The least-loaded server health
  - The Medevac tool is available at `http://support.citrix.com/article/CTX107935`

Using appropriate diagnostic steps

Every IT professional knows that issues occur. When issues occur, support personnel require traces and configuration information to identify the exact root cause of the reported issue. Using a common diagnostic tool consumes much time that is not always affordable for operations.

The Citrix Diagnostics Toolkit is a platform that comes with a collection of tools and automation options in an easy to use and organized format that closely resembles the look and feel of standard Windows applications, even though each tool is actually a separate application.

It has easy to use menus and shortcuts that allow you to quickly and successfully configure data collections and integrate with the other third-party tools for more robust debugging sessions.

The Citrix Diagnostics Toolkit is available at `http://support.citrix.com/article/CTX135075`.

There is another diagnostic tool for load balancing: the LBDiag—XenApp Load Balancing Diagnostic Tool.

LBDiag is a utility for diagnosing load balancing in XenApp 6 and later. LBDiag is available at `http://support.citrix.com/article/CTX124446`.

Performing a quick search on the Internet

After identifying the problem, if we don't know the solution, then we start searching it on the Internet. Now, at this moment, we should be clear about what we are looking for and where we will get our answers.

If we start our search in the wrong window, then the entire effort will be meaningless and that will directly impact our ability to solve that issue.

So, being a Citrix Administrator, we should know some web links where we can find an answer for the reported issue.

Let's take a look at some useful web links:

- Citrix Support: `http://support.citrix.com/`
- Citrix Products: `https://www.citrix.com/products.html`
- Citrix Product Documentation: `http://docs.citrix.com/`
- Citrix Blogs: `http://blogs.citrix.com/`

Using some additional methods to resolve the issue

Along with the Citrix technical support website, there are a lot of bloggers who have contributed to Citrix solutions for a long time. Such technical blogs can also help us to find the right solution for our problems.

There are also many discussion forums available on the Internet where Citrix Administrators, Citrix Engineers, Architects, and Citrix Technology Professionals share their experiences with others.

The CTP Awardees are available at `https://www.citrix.com/community/ctp/awardees.html`.

All of the awardees are continuously contributing their skills and research in desktop and application virtualization via their professional websites or by contributing to the Citrix community forums.

Following such blogs will help us to develop our troubleshooting and problem-solving skills.

Escalating the issue if required

After many attempts, you have finally decided to escalate the problem to the Citrix support team; before escalation, confirm whether this ends your involvement in this troubleshooting because escalating any issue is not the same as solving that issue.

You have to consider how long it will take the Citrix tech support team to solve the issue and how urgent the issue is to them. The Citrix support team will follow the same troubleshooting processes that we have already performed, as every issue get escalated level by level only.

If you are not able to solve the problem and a quick solution becomes time critical, then you need to come up with a workaround as a backup plan if the Citrix support team isn't able to address the issue in a timely manner. A temporary fix simplifies the problems experienced by the user, even if it does not address the root cause of the problem.

Examples of XenApp® issues

Now, we are well aware about what information we should collect before we begin troubleshooting XenApp issues. As per the best practices, all XenApp issues come under some categories, a node where we faced issues, and these categories are listed as:

- Citrix installation issues:
  - XenApp installation issues
  - Storefront installation issues
- XenApp component issues:
  - IMA service failures
  - ICA session connectivity problems
  - Data store corruption

- Profile issues:
  - ○ Windows user profile errors
  - ○ Folder redirection
  - ○ Group policy and registry problems

- Printing issues:
  - ○ Citrix Print Driver/Policy Failures
  - ○ Citrix Print Manager service crashes

Let's have some real-life examples of XenApp issues.

Citrix installation issues

Often, while installing Citrix XenApp roles such as XenApp Server Role, License Server, and Web Interface Server, we face various installation failures. Let's take a look at a few examples.

Scenario 1 – XenApp® installation fails

You are a Citrix Administrator installing Citrix XenApp 6.5 on a freshly installed Windows Server running 2008 R2. After a couple of steps, you get an error prompt **XenApp Failed**, as shown in the following screenshot:

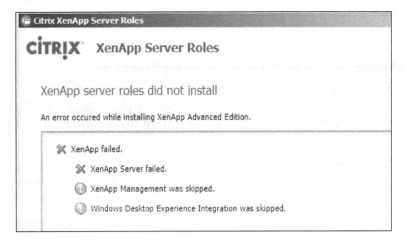

Troubleshooting

Let's begin the troubleshooting with the following steps:

1. Check whether there are any additional roles installed on Windows Server. Remove all server roles as the XenApp installer will install required server roles itself as part of the installation process.

2. Restart the VM and try again.

3. Check **Distributed Transaction Coordinator** and **Com+ System Application** Service state. We will see that it is running as expected.

4. Check whether any antivirus is enabled.

Resolution

Let's remove all XenApp components including all Microsoft Visual C++ redistributables from the Windows server. Remove the server from the domain and add it to a workgroup. Now try to install XenApp 6.5 and it should resolve the issue.

Conclusion

Sometimes, we prefer to use a local administrator account to ensure a smooth installation of the XenApp 6.5 version.

 Citrix has overcome this issue in the Citrix XenApp 6.5 Feature Pack 3.

Scenario 2 – StoreFront™ installation fails

An administrator supports a XenApp 5.0 farm consisting of 10 servers. The servers are physical and fitted with the same hardware. Users are connected to the server through published desktops. Now, the business team has a new requirement that they should be able to access these published desktops along with XenMobile applications, which are separately implemented.

To get this task accomplished, you as an administrator have decided to install a separate Storefront. But somehow, the installation failed as shown in the following screenshot:

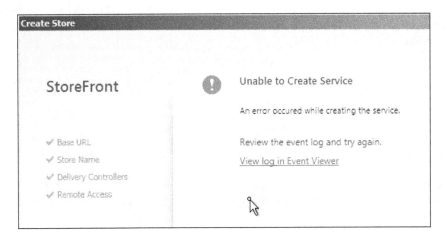

Troubleshooting

Let's begin the troubleshooting with the following steps:

1. Try uninstalling and reinstalling Storefront 2.5. However, you will notice that the issue still persists.
2. Try rebooting the server, but then you will notice the same error.
3. Check the firewall. If it is disabled, enable the firewall and try to reinstall.
4. Delete the directory at `C:\Program Files\Citrix\Receiver Storefront Directory`.
5. Install the full profile of .NET Framework 4.0.
6. Reboot the server and try again. However, the same issue arises.

Resolution

Finally, we decided to remove the entire server role and its components including IIS. After reboot, install only the IIS role and try to install Storefront again. It works!

Conclusion

While installing StoreFront, take a look at the following path if you run into any problems: `C:\inetpub\wwwroot\\Citrix\<storename>`.

The XenApp® component issues

There are many XenApp components that fail in the live production environment. Let's take a look at these examples.

The IMA service failure

This is a well-known issue of Citrix XenApp faced by every Citrix Administrator and Engineer in their career. In many stages, we have all faced IMA failure issues in a XenApp environment. For example:

- The IMA service fails to start at the initial configuration of XenApp 6.5
- Sometimes, IMA fails due to some changes by a XenApp Administrator
- Sometimes, the IMA service suddenly stops

Scenario

When starting IMA, the following error appears:

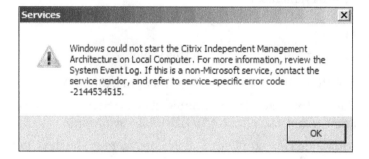

Troubleshooting

Try to start the service. Check the Event Viewer and you will find the details as seen in the following screenshot:

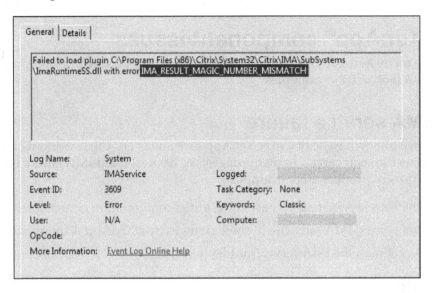

This issue occurs when there is an inconsistency between the data store's farm magic number and the IMA data hex key.

Resolution

Perform the following steps for resolving this issue:

1. In the install media, open dsview: `D:\support\debud\dsview.exe`

2. Open the `dsview.exe` file and double-click on **Server Neighborhoods**, **Farm name**, **Farm Data**, and **ATTRIBUTE-FarmMagic**

3. The FarmMagic Hex number must be consistent in the data store and in the registry. Note the hex number in the dsview.

4. Observe the hex number in the registry in `HKLM>SOFTWARE>Wow6432Node>Citrix>IMA>Data`. Note the key in the registry hive, `Data`.

 Making a wrong registry entry might cause an issue that might require a reinstall of the operating system.

The hex value should be the same as the value in the data store. Change the value if it is not the same:

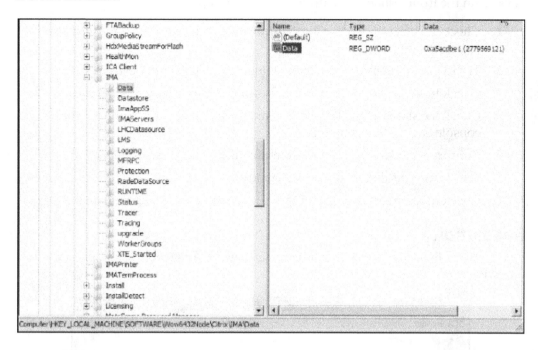

Conclusion

After the value has been changed to match the value in the FarmMagic value, start IMA.

For any kind of IMA issue, normally administrators prefer to use `dsmaint recreatelhc`.

Before recreating localhost cache, try to find out the exact cause of the IMA failure. Often, it gives different scenarios for troubleshooting.

The ICA session connectivity problem

Since the Citrix MetaFrame Presentation server, we often get user calls relating to the application launching and unusual disconnecting of ICA sessions. Let's see an example.

Scenario

Users are connected to a Citrix XenApp server and after some time get disconnected. There are no sessions visible on the server and the same symptoms apply while using Microsoft Remote Desktop.

Troubleshooting

Let's begin the troubleshooting with the following steps:

1. Check the behavior with a local administrator account and an enterprise domain admin account.

2. Try to ping the server, then try to telnet to the ICA port 1494.

3. Check to see whether any router, firewall, or proxy server is the cause.

4. Check the status of the loopback connection (ICA connection from the server console back to the same server).

5. Capture a network trace of a successful and unsuccessful connection.

6. Check after disabling Session Reliability.

7. Check that the server is listening on connection ports using `netstat`.

Resolution

Finally, we will decide to delete and recreate a new ICA listener, as shown in the following screenshot:

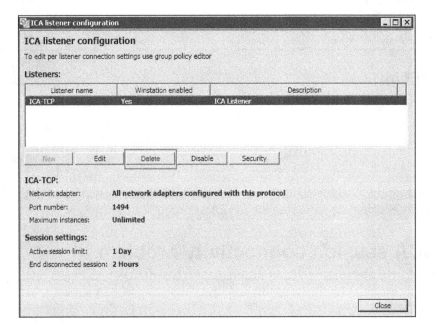

To configure the ICA listener, use the Citrix ICA Client Configuration Tool (`CtxICACfg.exe`).

Read this article to create a new ICA Listener. `http://support.`
`citrix.com/article/ctx125139`

We will be able to access the publish application and desktop after creating a new
ICA listener and rebooting the server.

Conclusion

The listener can get corrupted for a variety of reasons. An easy way to test if your
ICA listener is corrupted is to issue a telnet command to the server from a client
device or from the server itself.

Profile issues

User profiles are one of the key components of XenApp's application delivery
module. There are different types of profiles we have on Windows platforms,
such as local profiles, roaming profiles, and mandatory profiles.

Windows user profile errors

Let's see how to troubleshoot Windows profile issues.

Scenario

When the Citrix User Profile Manager Service is running on the server, if the users
do not have a local profile on the machine or a roaming profile in the domain, the
following error message is displayed when browsing the local drives:

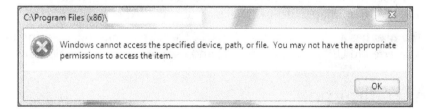

Symptoms

Here are some examples of profiling issues, especially while accessing local drives:

- An access denied error message appears when running `gpresult /r`, to a
  logged in user
- The access denied error message appears when browsing local drives

- The network adapter is shown as not connected
- It seems that the user environment was just partially loaded
- If you stop the UPM service on the XenDesktop virtual machine, you do not get the error message
- If users have a local or roaming profile, there is no issue and UPM performs as expected
- If users do not have a local or roaming profile and the UPM service is stopped, then they do not experience any errors
- If users do not have a roaming or local profile and the UPM service is RUNNING, they get an error
- Doing a procmon trace reveals that this is a permissions issue with `HKCU\Software\Classes` (or `HKU\SID_Classes`) where users do not have rights to their own hive
- This hive is copied from the default user profile, specifically the `usrclass.dat` file that resides in `C:\Users\Default\Appdata\local\microsoft\windows directory`

Resolution

You can resolve this issue by deleting `usrclass.dat` from the default user profile.

When this is deleted, the profile manager works without any issue as mentioned in the following list:

- The user does not have a local or roaming profile and the UPM service running. The roaming profile created user does not experience any errors.
- The user has a local profile, the UPM service is running, local profile moves to UPM roaming profile and the user does not experience any errors.
- The user has a roaming profile, the UPM service is running, roaming profile is converted to UPM roaming profile, and user does not experience any errors.

Folder redirection

Folder redirection is a common issue for Citrix administrators.

Scenario

Let's assume you are a Citrix administrator and have XenApp 6.5 running on 2008R2 RDS servers sitting in their own OU. One of the GPOs, which is applied to this OU is for **Folder Redirection**. You get the following error:

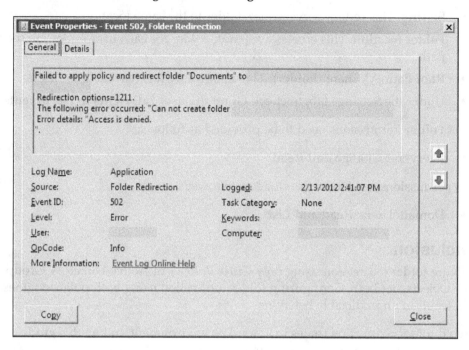

Troubleshooting

Let's begin the troubleshooting with the following steps:

1. Uncheck the option in the GPO settings to **Grant the user exclusive rights to Application Data** for the folder redirection. After disabling the GPO setting, you continue to get these messages.

2. Try restricting the child folders by NTFS permissions.

Resolution

The share folder was configured with the wrong permissions.

Check out the following settings of folder redirection:

- **Setting**: This redirects everyone's folder to the same location
- **Folder location**: This creates a separate folder for each user under the root path
- **Root Path (\\SharedFolder)**: This makes sure it is reachable for users
- Under the **Settings** tab, uncheck **Grant the user full rights to Documents**

Shared Folder Permissions need to be provided as follows:

- Everyone: **Change and Read**

NTFS permissions need to be provided as follows:

- Domain Users: **Read and List**

Conclusion

Configure folder redirection using only Citrix Policies or Active Directory Group Policy Objects, not both. Configuring folder redirection using both policy engines might result in unpredictable behavior.

To avoid folder redirection issues in a XenApp environment, follow this guide https://technet.microsoft.com/en-us/library/cc766489.

Group Policy and Registry problems

Most profile issues are caused by Group Policy and Registry corruption.

Scenario

When creating a XenApp policy within AppCenter and applying it to a worker group, it's very slow after clicking on **Browse** to bring up the list of worker groups:

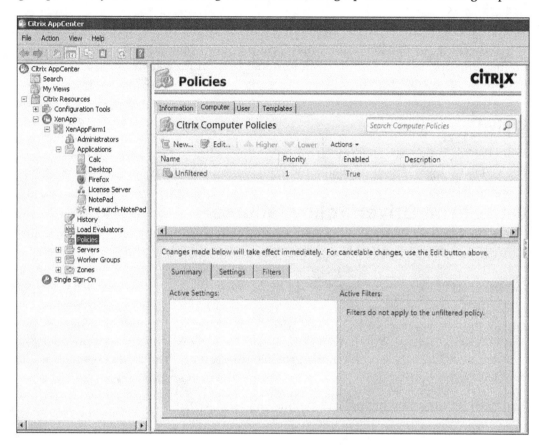

Troubleshooting

Let's begin the troubleshooting with the following steps:

1. Check that all Citrix XenApp policies are created with the Citrix Group Policy Management Console.

2. The user, computer, and other policy sections are not visible after starting the Citrix AppCenter console of XenApp 6.5.

Resolution

Upgrade all servers to version 1.7 of the Citrix Group Policy Management Console. All policies created with version 1.7 are visible again.

Conclusion

When checking the version of the Citrix Group Policy Management Console installed on the XenApp 6.5 controller, it was found that version 1.5 was installed and not version 1.7 as intended.

Printing issues

From the beginning, we are familiar with printing issues in the Citrix XenApp environment. Even with the MetaFrame Presentation server, we faced printing issues.

Citrix Print Driver/Policy failures

Let's have a look at an example on how to troubleshoot if Print Drivers failed on your XenApp Server.

Scenario

You have installed `CitrixUPClinet_SeflExtrator` on the XenApp 6.5 ZDCs and on the XenDesktop 5.6 DDCs, and also on the Windows 2008 R2 SP1 image, and Windows 7 image. You have installed `CitrixUPServer_SeflExtrator` on a Windows 2008 R2 SP1 server. On the Provisioning Server, Printer Management is enabled on the vDisks.

You have set the following policies on the DDC and XenApp ZDC:

- Machine Policy:
    - Universal Print Server is enabled
    - Universal Print Server Print Data Stream Port is set to `7229`
    - Universal Print Server Web Service HTTP/SOAP port is set to `8080`
- User Policy:
    - **Default Printer**: Set the default printer to the client's main printer
    - **Universal Print Driver usage**: Use the printer model-specific drivers only if UP is unavailable

We get the following message when trying to add a printer through the print server share:

Windows couldn't connect to the printer. Check the printer name and try again. If this is a network printer, make sure that the print is turned on, and that the printer address is correct.

Troubleshooting

Let's begin the troubleshooting with the following steps:

1. Check the required Hotfix for the environment and install.

2. Verify that port 8080 is only assigned to UPS.

3. Change the XML port to 8085.

4. Run stressprint.exe from the server to test the drivers to ensure compatibility.

5. Try this article after some research: http://support.citrix.com/article/ CTX134758.

Still the same problem persists.

Resolution

Add the LimitRequestFieldSize 65535 line either before #Citrix_Begin or after #Citrix_End; lines in between get rewritten at service startup.

Conclusion

Clustering the Citrix Universal Print Server is currently not supported.

Citrix Print Manager Service crashes

Citrix Printer Manager Service cpsvc.exe is a very important service for performing printing operations in the Citrix XenApp environment. Let's see how to troubleshoot if this service has issues.

Scenario

You have a new XenApp 6.5 farm with Hotfix Rollup 1 installed. The Citrix Print Manager Service crashes several times a day on your different servers. This probably happens a total of about 5-7 times a day among your 4 servers.

It seems that when Windows XP clients log on to the servers, this service crashes right after the system logs on. The clients are running Citrix Receiver Enterprise 3.4 (13.4.0.25). Your farm is set to only use Citrix UPD:

- In the system log you get:

  ° **Event ID 7034**: The Citrix Print Manager Service terminated unexpectedly

- In the application log you get:

  ° **Event ID 1000**: You'll see the following error:

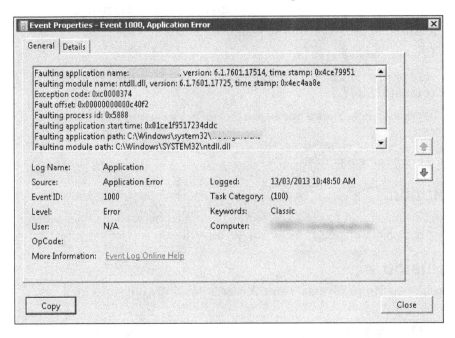

Troubleshooting

Let's begin the troubleshooting with the following steps:

1. Your XP clients have different printers/drivers; some are USB and some are the network.

2. We try to restart the print manager service but did not succeed.

3. Run CDFTrace to see what is causing the service to crash.

4. Analyze the output to understand if it was a driver issue, print job, and so on, at the core of the problem.

Resolution

After some research, we come to know that after installing Hotfix Rollup Pack 2 issues get resolved.

Conclusion

If printing is core to the business and needs to be done from multiple locations, then a combination of a third-party print management tool and Citrix UPD would normally be the best way to deliver an effective printing solution.

To identify print driver problems, we can use Citrix's Print Detective Tool. This is available at `http://support.citrix.com/article/CTX116474?_ga=1.249147394.487791637.1439651886`.

Printing is one of the well-known issues for all Citrix Administrators. Whenever we face print-related issues in our Citrix Environment, there are some basic things that we should follow when troubleshooting.

For example:

- Try to restart the Print Spooler and Print Manager services
- Run `stressprint.exe`
- Check the compatibility of end users' Printer with Citrix XenApp

To know more about XenApp Printing, follow these links:

- *Citrix Printing Planning Guide*: `http://support.citrix.com/servlet/KbServlet/download/32205-102-696273/Printing%20Planning%20Guide.pdf`
- *Introduction to Windows Printing Concepts*: `http://support.citrix.com/proddocs/topic/xenapp65-admin/ps-printing-network-basics.html`
- *Configuring and Maintaining XenApp Printing*: `http://support.citrix.com/proddocs/topic/xenapp65-admin/ps-printing-configuring-wrapper.html`

Summary

In this chapter, we covered how to prepare for troubleshooting, what the basic troubleshooting processes are, how to identify and analyze any XenApp problem, and how to reach the exact cause of XenApp problems.

At the end of this chapter, you learned some troubleshooting tips for some well-known XenApp issues.

In the next chapter, we will see more examples of other Citrix XenApp components that play an important role in delivering applications to end users through multiple platforms.

Troubleshooting Other Issues

In the previous chapter, we saw how to identify and troubleshoot XenApp issues. In this chapter, we will see the issues related to other XenApp components.

The following topics will be covered in this chapter:

- Provisioning Services issues
- StoreFront issues
- NetScaler issues
- Infrastructure issues

Provisioning Services issues

Provisioning Services plays an important role in large-scale deployments. Using Provisioning Services, we can quickly roll out the changes to the complete XenApp farm or XenDesktop VDI environment.

Provisioning Services streams the master image to a user device. It does not require a hypervisor to do this, so you can use it to host a physical machine.

When Provisioning Services is included in a site, it communicates with the controller to provide users with resources.

Citrix Provisioning Services gives single instance virtual desktop management. That means you only have to update a single image that will then stream to thousands of desktops. You just have to install new software on the master image, and to get it streamed to all other servers we just need to reboot them all. Once all these servers are rebooted, then automatically, the new software will be available on all these servers.

When we update the PVS master image, it creates a version of vDisk, which gives versioning control. As a result, having a version of vDisk, we can roll back all unwanted changes to their previous state.

Having Provisioning Services implemented with the XenApp and XenDesktop environment reduces the troubleshooting time and efforts. For example, if you are having an issue with a desktop, by rebooting it that desktop will stream with vDisk as on the first boot.

Provisioning Services advantages

The following are the advantages of Provisioning Services:

- It minimizes the overall time it takes to update all XenApp/XenDesktop servers
- Using Provisioning Services, we can quickly expand our XenApp farm
- It maximizes overall server uptime
- Provisioning Services will give you a quick rollback mechanism
- It will reduce the overall storage space requirement
- Within one reboot, we can easily deliver the server updates to any number of servers

Let's have a look at the issues we may face with Citrix Provisioning Services.

Scenario 1 – BOOTMGR is missing

You are using the PVS imaging wizard to import a vDisk into a PVS server and you get an error prompt while rebooting the machine. After reboot, PXE works properly, but you get an error prompt and booting stops:

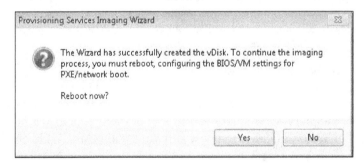

Troubleshooting

Proceed with the following steps:

1. Remount the vDisk, open the disk partition, and set it to active.
2. Check the NIC driver on the target device.
3. Go to the virtual machine properties in **Virtual Device Node**, and free up the position **0:0**.
4. Move the existing disk to any other position.
5. Reboot the machine again.
6. It worked with a single virtual disk, so unplug the second virtual disk.

Conclusion

Citrix Provisioning Services 5.6 Service Pack 2 supports only a single virtual disk.

Scenario 2 – operating system error with PVS

You tried to create vDisk on a shared storage, which failed with an error prompt as follows:

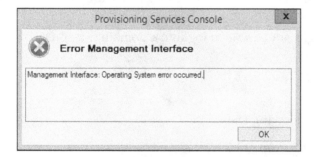

Resolution

Run the following command in PowerShell on all PVS servers:

```
Set-ItemProperty -Path
"HKLM:\SYSTEM\CurrentControlSet\Services\LanmanWorkstation\Parameters"
RequiresSecureNegotiate -Value 0 -Force
```

This can be caused by the secure dialect negotiation; this is a feature available in MSB 3.0 for Windows Server 2012 in which error responses by SMB servers are incorrectly signed. If the SMB client doesn't receive a properly signed certificate, then the connection will drop resulting in the preceding error.

As per Microsoft documentations, some file servers have not supported this type of feature, resulting in failure messages.

Read about *SMB3 Secure Dialect Negotiation* at `http://blogs.msdn.com/b/openspecification/archive/2012/06/28/smb3-secure-dialect-negotiation.aspx`.

Scenario 3 – the effect of Daylight saving time on Citrix Provisioning Services

As PVS is a streaming technology, it is affected whenever there is a change in **Daylight saving time (DST)**.

Users might face the following issues due to Daylight saving time changes:

- In the desktop (published by XenApp HSD), time might not be shown
- The desktop might have failed to register with the XenApp Desktop delivery controller
- Users might not be able to log into a domain due to DC trust relationship issues

Resolution

Proceed with the following steps:

1. Go to the XenApp golden image.
2. Open the PVS delivered images in the read or write mode.
3. Run the following command in Command Prompt:

   ```
   W32tm /resync /nowait
   ```

4. Again, set the image back to read only mode.

5. Reboot all the delivered desktops and servers once you make preceding changes.

StoreFront™ issues

Citrix StoreFront is an enterprise application store that helps mobile users to work from anywhere and any device. StoreFront really improves the enterprise level security and makes the administration part easier by simplifying the deployment part of XenApp and XenDesktop multi-tenant and multisite environments.

Citrix StoreFront gives users on-demand access to applications, desktops, and data.

Scenario 1 – cannot complete your request

An often-encountered, well-known issue in StoreFront is when you attempt to access the StoreFront site and get an error prompt stating **Cannot complete your request. You can log on and try again, or contact your help desk for assistance:**

Solutions

If you see the preceding error, **Cannot complete your request**, then there is the possibility of a StoreFront URL being different from the actual certificate bound in IIS.

Once you change the matching certificate, then you should be able to log on to the StoreFront site.

Scenario 2 – StoreFront™ upgrade issue from 2.6 to 3.0

As a Citrix administrator, you upgraded Citrix StoreFront Version 2.6 to 3.0. It was installed on Windows Server 2012 R2 and was affected by **Certified Trust List** (CTL) changes. In the event log, you receive continuous event prompts every 5 minutes:

```
Log Name:        Citrix Delivery Services
Source:          Citrix Credential Wallet Service
Date:            07/07/2014 1:11:11 PM
Event ID:        9
Task Category:   (2302)
Level:           Warning
Keywords:        Classic
User:            N/A
Computer:        %DDC%
Description:
The replication channel failed to open.
Synchronisation is disabled.
```

Cause

In the upgrade process, the **Credential Wallet Service (CWS)** configuration file is incorrectly modified.

Solution

Windows Server 2012 does not send a list of trusted CAs during the SSL handshake, resulting in the Linux client failing to provide a client certificate. The changes to Windows 2012 Server are documented at *What's New in TLS/SSL (Schannel SSP)*.

Windows Receiver clients will work if a CTL list is not sent to the client. For the Linux Receiver client, it is necessary to enable the CTL list.

The following registry edit is required:

HKEY_LOCAL_MACHINE\SYSTEM\CurrentControlSet\Control\SecurityProviders\ SCHANNEL

Value name: SendTrustedIssuerList

Value type: REG_DWORD

Value data: 1 (True)

Scenario 3 – Cannot contact Store

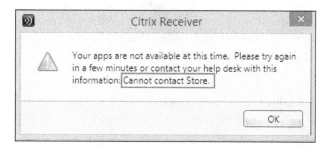

The environment details are as follows:

- **XenApp Version**: XenApp 7.0
- **StoreFront Version**: 2.0
- **Receiver Version**: 4.0
- **Citrix NetScaler**: No
- **Access Gateway**: No
- **Authentication Type**: Username and password

The Citrix Storefront website works properly, but when tried from a desktop using the Citrix Receiver 4.0, we get the preceding error.

Troubleshooting

Proceed with the following steps:

1. On the StoreFront server, in the **Authentication** node, for trusted domains, verify that NetBIOS and UPN suffixes are added to the list.

2. On the client device, in **Task Manager**, verify that the ssonsvr.exe process is running.

3. Check that, for trusted sites, we only need the FQDN added and probably not /Citrix/Store.

4. Check the certificate.

Solution

Finally, after checking a server certificate that was self-signed, we created a new server certificate by requesting a properly signed certificate from the CA. Then, we uploaded it on the web server and added the root CA certificate on the client machine. We tested the login part and it works fine.

If you don't want to waste a lot of time troubleshooting such a minor mistake, then before implementing your Citrix StoreFront in your environment, follow the best practices published by Citrix. It will definitely minimize the post implementation pain.

Follow this implementation guide of Citrix StoreFront at `http://support.citrix.com/article/CTX133185`.

NetScaler® issues

Citrix NetScaler is another important component in the XenApp and XenDesktop environment.

In *Chapter 1, Basic Troubleshooting Methodology*, we have already seen the uses and advantages of NetScaler Gateway in a XenApp environment.

Scenario 1 – user not able to change the password

Users who access the web interface on NetScaler are not able to change their expired password on login.

The environment details are as follows:

- **Citrix XenApp**: XenApp 6.5 Enterprise Edition
- **Citrix NetScaler**: NetScaler Software release 9.3 nCore
- **StoreFront / Web interface**: Citrix web interface

  ```
  "Unable to change expired password using web interface on Citrix
  NetScaler."
  ```

Troubleshooting

Proceed with the following steps:

1. For testing, try to configure a direct PNAgent site to access web interface for thin clients on NetScaler.

2. Verify the `webinterface.conf` file and update it as follows:

```
Default Configuration
AllowUserPasswordChange=Never
PNAChangePasswordMethod=Direct-Only

Change To
AllowUserPasswordChange=Expired-Only
PNAChangePasswordMethod=Proxy
```

3. Save the changes on NetScaler, and try to access the site and see if you get the same error.

4. After saving this configuration, observe that the `config.xml` file did not replicate the changes.

5. Now take network packet traces:

```
POST /Citrix/PNAgent/XD/change_password.jsp HTTP/1.1
Content-Type: application/x-www-form-urlencoded
Host: pna.ns.example.com
User-Agent: WTOS/1.0
Content-Length: 311
Connection: Keep-Alive
Cache-control: no-cache
```

6. You will see the HTTP 500 Internal Server Error with the following details:

```
HTTP/1.1 500 Internal Server Error
Set-Cookie: JSESSIONID=BD6D583BFEE853FA6674568A9EF915C1; Path=/Citrix/PNAgent/XD
Pragma: no-cache
Cache-Control: no-store
Expires: Mon, 01 Jan 1990 12:00:00 GMT


DPErrorId: CharlotteErrorOther
DPError:
Content-Type: text/xml;charset=UTF-8
Content-Length: 50
Date: Tue, 27 Mar 2012 07:42:25 GMT
Connection: close
Server: Apache
```

This error occurred because the ASP.NET and JSP implementations of web interface differed in how they expected to receive XML from the client.

Resolution

To overcome this issue, we need to update the `webinterface.conf` file as per the following changes:

```
AllowUserPasswordChange=Expired-Only
PNAChangePasswordMethod=Proxy
The engineers also requested the customer to add
the following rewrite policy and bind the rewrite the policy to AGEE vserver:
add rewrite policy testpolicy "HTTP.REQ.URL.CONTAINS(\"change_password\")" test_insert2
add rewrite action test_insert2 insert_before_all
"HTTP.REQ.BODY(5)" "\"xmlDocument=\"" -search "text(\"<?xml\")"
```

After applying the preceding changes, the user is now able to change their password and get logged on again with the newly changed password.

Scenario 2 – Cannot start desktop or app

In the past, we were using the web interface and now, in order to support Chromebook and Windows RT desktops, we want to upgrade to Citrix StoreFront. Similarly, we have built the new StoreFront environment, but while accessing published applications and desktops we get an error stating **Cannot start desktop or app**:

The environment details are as follows:

- **Citrix XenApp**: XenApp 6.5
- **Citrix StoreFront**: StoreFront 2.6
- **NetScaler Gateway**: NetScaler 10.0

Troubleshooting

Proceed with the following steps:

1. Try to access the StoreFront website internally and find the applications that are being launched as expected.
2. Check whether STA configured in the NetScaler Gateway is the same as configured in the StoreFront configuration.
3. The problem still persists.
4. Remove the STA entries from the StoreFront server and add them again as mentioned in Citrix Best Practice for StoreFront.

Solution

Finally, we got to the cause and found that STA was wrongly configured at the StoreFront end. Rolling back with the correct inputs solved the problem.

Scenario 3 – Citrix XenApp® 6.0, NetScaler® VPN access, and the DNS issue

We have a created a virtual server on Citrix AGEE, which allows VPN access with split tunneling to our internal environment. NetScaler is located in the DMZ and the DNS server is located internally. Required ports are opened. Now, users connected to the VPN tunnel are not able to resolve the internal hosts.

Troubleshooting

Proceed with the following steps:

1. Add the DNS suffix to Citrix NetScaler and on the access gateway.
2. Add the internal DNS server as the root name server on Citrix NetScaler.
3. Check the specified range of IP addresses from the DMZ network to be used on the Access Gateway.
4. Try to ping the DNS server from NSIP.

Solution

Perhaps it should be stated that, after troubleshooting the network, possible firewall issues can be identified.

Opening ICMP packets between the NetScaler SNIP and the DNS server solved the preceding issue.

In such kind of scenarios, we found that customers who belong to the banking and finance domain have multiple firewalls and security points, which add unwanted troubles in the investigation process. Sometimes, data protection agents (such as DLP Agent) also cause big difficulties in Citrix troubleshooting.

Scenario 4 – Unable to proceed from the login page while using NetScaler™ 10.1 and Citrix XenApp® 7.6

The customer deploys NetScaler Gateway 10.1 for external access to Citrix XenApp 7.6. At the time of logging, the customer can redirect to Citrix Receiver's login page, but when they enter login credentials and click on the **Login** button, nothing is happening on the screen.

Troubleshooting

Proceed with the following steps:

1. Try with the Access Gateway FQDN and IP address.
2. In Event Viewer, look for the following event logs:
   - Task category 1005:

```
The AG Web Service at: https://<AccessGatewayFQDN>
/CitrixAuthService/AuthService.asmx failed with the following error.
This endpoint will be ignored until: 16/4/15 10:18:38 AM
Citrix.DeliveryServices.Authentication.CitrixAGBasic.
Exceptions.AGCommunicationException,
Citrix.DeliveryServices.Authentication.CitrixAGBasic,
Version=2.6.0.0, Culture=neutral, PublicKeyToken=null
A communication error occurred while attempting
to contact the NetScaler Gateway authentication service at
https://<AccessGatewayFQDN>/CitrixAuthService/AuthService.asmx.
Check that the authentication service is running.
```

    °   Task category 3001:

```
A CitrixAGBasic Login request has failed.
Citrix.DeliveryServicesClients.Authentication.AG.AGAuthenticatorException,
Citrix.DeliveryServicesClients.Authentication,
Version=2.6.0.0, Culture=neutral, PublicKeyToken=null
Authenticate encountered an exception.
```

As per the event, StoreFront is not able to connect to the callback URL.

Solution

On the Citrix StoreFront server, open a browser and point it to `https://CallbackFQDN`.

Now we can see the login page and no certificate errors.

Infrastructure issues

In Citrix XenApp, to run smooth operations, we should definitely consider all those infrastructure components which play an important role in building an enterprise-grade Citrix XenApp environment.

Even unknowingly, we might miss an infrastructure component while designing or building the XenApp architecture. This might result in pain for our operations team.

Before any XenApp implementation, if we follow the proper solution path, then our XenApp farm will work smoothly after the deployment.

Let's see some examples of infrastructure related issues from a Citrix XenApp environment.

Domain Controller issues with Citrix XenApp®

The Domain Controller is one of the most important components in the Citrix XenApp environment for user authentication.

Scenario 1 – Applications are unable to launch from one domain in the multi-domain XenApp® environment

In the following diagram, users from the Mumbai domain are able to launch the applications successfully; however, users from the London domain are unable to launch any applications.

We have an architecture view of the multi-domain XenApp environment in the following diagram:

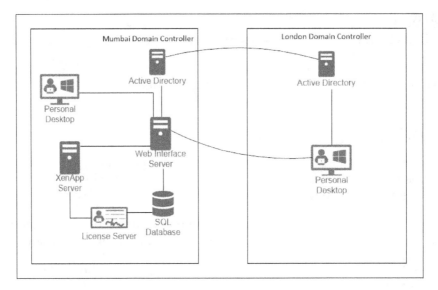

Troubleshooting

Proceed with the following steps:

1. Verify that all the required Citrix and Microsoft hotfixes are installed on all farm servers.

2. Check that the Citrix Legacy client is being used to connect to the published application.

3. Check the status of the Profile Management Service. It should be in the starting mode.

4. Check the event logs on all the XenApp servers. Ensure that none of the servers contains any errors.

5. For testing purposes, disable all the printing policies and client logon scripts.

6. For testing purposes, try to launch applications from the Mumbai domain; applications will be launched successfully. When trying to launch applications from the London domain, the application fails.

7. Confirm that a bi-directional trust is set up between the Mumbai and London forests.

8. Check that all group policies are applied successfully on all XenApp Servers.

9. Using Microsoft Terminal Services, publish the same applications and try to access them. This should resolve the issue.

Resolution

If an application is not started on time, that session automatically exits. In this scenario, the session is terminated because it took a long time to validate the credentials between the two domains.

To set the length of the time, we need to make some changes in the registry, as follows:

```
HKEY_LOCAL_MACHINE\SYSTEM\CurrentControlSet\Control\Citrix\wfshell\TWI

Value Name: LogoffCheckerStartupDelayInSeconds

Type: REG_DWORD

Value: An integer for the length of time to wait for application start
(10 Hexadecimal Recommended)
```

Scenario 2 – slow login on Citrix XenApp sites with Read Only Domain Controller

XenApp users reported that they are experiencing slowness while logging in to XenApp sites with **Read Only Domain Controller (RODC)**.

Cause

The RODC triggers **Active Directory Service Interface** (**ADSI**) connections resulting in a slow login and Windows logon screen to happen.

Troubleshooting

Proceed with the following steps:

1. Try to remove or block as many GPOs as possible.
2. Try to remove or disable your logon script.
3. Also, verify that no one has grassed anything into `usrlogon.cmd` on the XenApp server.
4. Disable Citrix Client Drive Mapping.
5. Disable Citrix Client Printer Mapping.
6. Disable Roaming Profiles.
7. Verify that there are no entries in DNS or in your hosts file on the XenApp server.

To get over this issue, we can switch away from RODC on XenApp sites where we are facing login issues.

Resolution

The Citrix support team has already found the root cause for this issue, and depending on the operating system, the Citrix Hotfixes are available as follows:

- **CTX133801 (Hotfix XAE500R01W2K8066)**: For Citrix XenApp 5.0 for Windows Server 2008 x86
- **CTX133804 (Hotfix XAE500R01W2K8X64063)**: For Citrix XenApp 5.0 for Windows Server 2008 x64
- **CTX133760 (Hotfix XA600R01W2K8R2X64047)**: For Citrix XenApp 6.0 for Windows Server 2008 R2 - English
- **CTX134055 (Hotfix XA650R01W2K8R2X64011)**: For Citrix XenApp 6.5 for Windows Server 2008 R2 - English

For more information about this issue, visit `http://support.citrix.com/article/CTX133873`.

The SQL database mirroring issue with Citrix XenApp®

Using SQL database mirroring in the Citrix XenApp environment improves its disaster recovery capabilities.

Scenario

We have a Citrix XenApp 6.0 environment with 3 SQL servers (Principal, Mirror, and Witness), which is to be used for database mirroring on Microsoft SQL servers 2005. As per the test, the mirroring is working fine, but the Citrix XenApp failover is not working as expected.

We are getting an IMA error stating **Cannot connect to database**. The connection gets lost when we try to start the failover, as shown in the screenshot, for example:

```
ODBC
DRIVER=SQL Native Client
UID="SQL Admin id"
Failover_Partner="Mirror Server"
DATABASE=XenappTest
WSID="Server Name"
APP=Citrix IMA
SERVER="principal Server"
```

Troubleshooting

Proceed with the following steps:

1. Change the `MF20.dsn` file to reflect the failover partner on all the XenApp servers.

2. Follow these steps:

   ```
   dsmaint config /user: ABCnetwork\administrator
   /pwd:Passw0rd101 /dsn:"C:\Program Files
   (x86)\Citrix\Independent Management Architecture\mf20.dsn"
   DSMAINT RECREATELHC
   RESTART IMASERVICE
   ```

Solution

As per Citrix's recommendations, a data store timeout will be ready before continuing. For more details, read this Citrix article at `http://support.citrix.com/article/CTX107708`.

Follow these steps for the solution:

1. Stop the Citrix IMA service using the command `net stop imaservice`.

2. Install the Microsoft SQL Native Client.

3. To download Microsoft SQL Native Client, follow this link `https://msdn.microsoft.com/en-us/sqlserver/aa937733.aspx`.

4. Edit the **Data Source Name (DSN)** as follows:

```
ODBC
\\ DRIVER= {SQL Native Client} \\ UID=administrator
\\ Trusted_Connection=Yes \\DATABASE =XA DS
\\ WSID=CTXXA02 \\ APP=Citrix IMA
\\ SERVER=CTXSQ02 \\ Failover_Partner=CTXSQ01
\\ Description=ds
```

5. Once done, start the Citrix IMA service using the command `net start imaservice`.

6. Install the SQL Server Native Client on all the XenApp servers.

References

Some useful links for SQL database mirroring with Citrix XenApp are as follows:

- *Using SQL Database Mirroring to Improve Citrix XenApp Server Farm Disaster Recovery Capabilities*: `http://support.citrix.com/article/CTX111311`

- *Changing a Production XenApp 7.x Site to use SQL Mirroring*: `http://carlwebster.com/changing-production-xendesktop-7x-site-use-sql-mirroring/`

- *Troubleshoot Database Mirroring Configuration (SQL Server)*: `https://msdn.microsoft.com/en-IN/library/ms189127.aspx`

Summary

In this chapter, we covered how to identify and troubleshoot the components that play an important role in XenApp's end-user computing architecture. We saw how to troubleshoot with Provisioning Services, NetScaler Gateway, Citrix StoreFront, and other infrastructure components.

In the next chapter, we will see how to improve performance and optimize the Citrix XenApp environment.

5
Monitoring and Optimizing

In the previous chapter, we saw how to identify and troubleshoot using the components that play an important role in XenApp's end user computing architecture. In this chapter, we will see how to monitor and optimize the Citrix XenApp infrastructure using various toolkits.

The following topics will be covered in this chapter:

- Using EdgeSight
- Using Director
- Other monitoring tools
- Optimizing Citrix XenApp

Using EdgeSight®

Citrix EdgeSight is a performance monitoring and availability management solution. It is primarily used to monitor hosted applications, desktops, devices, sessions, license usage, and real-time network analysis.

Citrix EdgeSight allows you to define, examine, and categorize a resolution for performance issues from a single user interface. You can use EdgeSight to show notifications of performance problems, show hardware and software changes on systems, show system performance metrics over time, and show resources being used by the servers and systems.

Citrix EdgeSight allows support engineers to identify which server a user is logged on to and then show significant performance information. Also, an extensive range of network related reports is available that provide information about traffic in and out of the ICA client. Citrix EdgeSight helps to identify application issues (such as slowness or crashes) and identifies and defines whether the issue is a Citrix-related issue or a result of network issues such as network delay, web errors, or high round-trip times.

Citrix EdgeSight helps you solve Citrix environmental problems; it can also help you in planning and implementing your Citrix infrastructure. With Citrix EdgeSight, you can manage application versioning, capacity planning, roll out in-house applications and also implement licensing and compliance policies.

Citrix EdgeSight gives information on how applications and servers are utilized and also license details for your environments.

Citrix EdgeSight® components

The following are the key components of Citrix EdgeSight:

- EdgeSight Agents
- EdgeSight Server
- EdgeSight Server Console
- Citrix License Server

There are other components that are also required when monitoring the virtual desktop environment.

For more details on system requirements, visit the following link: `https://docs. citrix.com/en-us/edgesight/5-4/es-system-reqs-54.html`.

The Citrix EdgeSight components and its roles are as follows:

- **EdgeSight for XenApp Agent**: EdgeSight monitors the performance of Citrix XenApp Server. Multiple versions of the agent are provided to accommodate different XenApp versions.
- **EdgeSight Server**: This displays performance data for monitored devices.
- **EdgeSight for Endpoints Agent**: This monitors the performance of physical clients.
- **EdgeSight Active Application Monitoring (AAM) Components**: This performs a manual test to monitor the end-user experience of applications in XenApp and Presentation Server environments.
- **EdgeSight Agent Database Server**: This stores performance data for agents monitoring virtual desktops.
- **EdgeSight for Virtual Desktops Agent**: This monitors the performance of instances of XenDesktop 4.0 or later.

The following figure shows the relationship between the preceding components and its systems:

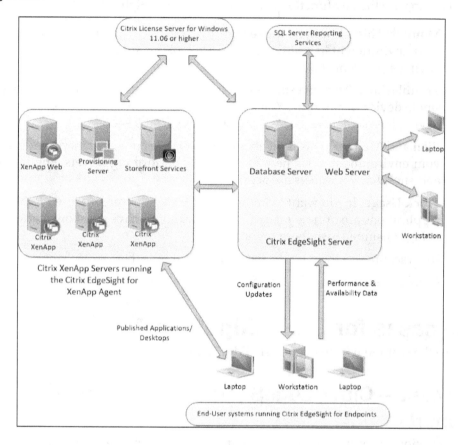

With EdgeSight, you can monitor the health of the entire Citrix XenApp Farm, get notified when an application crashes, and find out when there is a network problem before all your users call your service desk. You can see the most frequently used applications in your XenApp environment and which users are using these applications. You can see the license utilization for all your Citrix products and it will be easy to find out wherever it requires additional licenses.

You can see which application consumes the most of your system resources and see which application has had the most problems over the last few months. You can even figure out why it takes a long time for a user to launch a published application.

For those who are technically savvy, the detailed real-time performance counters on XenApp servers, virtual devices, or endpoints will allow you to troubleshoot problems that a user is currently facing.

Key functional areas of Citrix EdgeSight®

The following are the key functional areas of Citrix EdgeSight:

- **Monitor**: This allows you to see performance and availability problems in your environment in real time. If you are looking around to see if anyone is having a problem start here.

- **Troubleshoot**: This investigates performance and stability problems on a single device in real time. You will suspect that there is a problem with a device, application, or user before using the troubleshooters.

- **Plan and Manage**: This is all about performance and constancy trends in your environment. Look here for the worst performing servers, applications, and sites that your users are accessing.

- **Track Usage**: If you want to know what the most frequently used Published Applications are or how many Citrix licenses you have and how many are being consumed, use these reports.

- **Browse**: Browse through the list of historical reports.

- **Configure**: These are the EdgeSight settings pages.

Use cases for Citrix EdgeSight®

Let's see the real-life use cases of Citrix EdgeSight.

Use case – Citrix EdgeSight® for application support

An application support contains understanding resource usage, performance trends, the network's effect of the application, and also, understanding the ongoing maintenance, such as installing important patches and updates.

Fundamental scenarios for application support

The following are the fundamental scenarios of application support:

- Resource usage, performance trends, network effect
- Patching and updating Citrix hosted applications
- Crash analysis of in-house application development
- Checking version compatibility and its impact

In every organization, application issues are usually reported by the end users or prompted by real-time alerts. The user's session that reported the issue can be used to conclude on which computer the application is running at the time of the error prompt.

Use case – Citrix EdgeSight® for issue resolution

Any technical issues typically start with a symptom such as error pop-ups, network connectivity problems, blue screens, or slow response time. Once a warning sign gets noted, then the cause of the problem should be understood and then resolved.

Key scenarios for issue resolution

The following are the key scenarios for issue resolution:

- What event happened in that situation?
- What is the device status at the time of the trigger?
- Is there any change in asset?
- Are any processes demanding a lot of resources?
- Are there any other issues with the servers that could be exacerbating the symptoms reported?

Use case – Citrix EdgeSight® for capacity planning and device health

Performance statistics gives you information about what resources are being used and where the problem might be occurring. Device reliability gives you information about process errors, software version compatibility, and overall device health. Citrix EdgeSight Agent collects the asset data about the device it is running on, such as the size of hard drive, CPU speed, physical RAM installed, and type of network card. Use this information to determine whether the device can support a new application or operating system upgrade in its current state.

Key scenarios for capacity planning and device health

The following are the key scenarios for capacity planning and device health:

- Support for new technologies, such as Windows 8.1 or Windows 10
- Application deployment
- Device stability
- Device upgrade and planning

Using Citrix® Director

Citrix Director allows Citrix administrators to handle a large number of applications and a large desktop infrastructure. It provides a web-based interface to the entry-level helpdesk engineers to help users and accomplish routine maintenance activities without providing them full access to the Citrix XenApp or XenDesktop console. Using Citrix Director, helpdesk engineers can view the user sessions and can act upon delivering first or second level support by troubleshooting user issues.

Citrix Director is a tool that can be used to troubleshoot user issues before they become system critical as well as perform support jobs for end users. Citrix Director provides different views of the interface personalized to particular Citrix administrators. Citrix XenDesktop permissions define what is displayed and what commands are available.

Citrix Director permits support engineers/administrators to search for the user reporting an issue and show the activity related to that particular user, such as the status of the user's processes and applications. Support personnel can resolve issues quickly by performing actions such as closing an unresponsive application or process, restarting the machine, resetting the user profile, or shadowing operations on the user's machine.

In disparity, full administrators can see and manage the entire farm site and can perform the required commands for multiple users and machines. The dashboard gives a summary of the significant features of a Citrix deployment such as the status of user logins, number of user sessions, and an overview of the site infrastructure. This information gets updated every minute. If issues happen, then the details about the type and number of failures that have happened appear automatically on the dashboard.

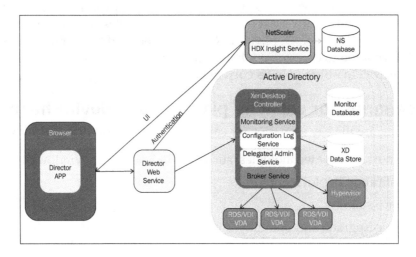

Deploying and configuring Citrix® Director

By default, Citrix Director gets installed as a website on the delivery controller. For prerequisites and other details, refer to the following link: `http://support.citrix.com/article/CTX200330`.

Citrix Director 7.6.100 is not companionable with Citrix XenApp deployments earlier than 6.5 or XenDesktop deployments earlier than 7.

When Citrix Director is used in an environment containing more than one site, be sure to synchronize the system clocks on all the servers where Controllers, Director, and other core components are installed. Otherwise, the sites might not display correctly in Director.

> If you want to monitor XenApp 6.5 in addition to XenApp 7.5 or XenDesktop 7.x sites, it's highly recommended to install Citrix Director on a separate server from the Director console that is used to monitor Citrix XenApp sites.

This is the snapshot of Director's dashboard:

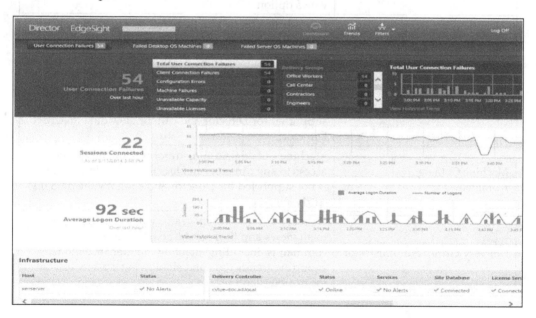

Administrator roles and their permissions in Citrix® Director

Administrator role	Permissions in Director
Helpdesk Administrator	Helpdesk administrator can access the user details views and view the objects that the administrator is delegated to manage. Helpdesk admins can also shadow a user's session and perform the required commands for that user. They can also perform maintenance mode operations for end users. Helpdesk admins can use power control options only for Desktop OS Machines not for Server OS Machines.
Read-Only Administrator	Read-Only Administrators are able to access all views and see all objects in detailed scopes as well as global information. They are able to download reports from HDX channels and can export Trends data from the Trends view using the Export option. They cannot execute any other command or change anything in the views option.
Full Administrator	Full Administrator will have full access to all views and can execute all commands including enabling maintenance mode, exporting trends data, and shadowing a user's session for troubleshooting.
Host Administrator	Host Administrator will not have any access to any directory in Director. This administrator is not supported for Director and cannot view data on Citrix Director.
Machine Catalog Administrator	Machine Catalog Administrator will not have any access to any directory in Director. This administrator is not supported for Director and cannot view data on Citrix Director.
Delivery Group Administrator	Delivery Group Administrator will have full access to all views and they can be able to execute all commands, including enabling maintenance mode, exporting trends data and shadowing a user's session for troubleshooting.

Monitoring with Citrix® Director

Citrix Administrators and helpdesk engineers can monitor Citrix XenApp and XenDesktop sites with Citrix Director, where administrators can access the configuration logging database, or by using the site's monitor service's API, with the OData protocol.

Administrators can monitor the following:

- Historical trends
- Infrastructure
- Connection failures
- Session usage
- User sessions
- Login performance
- Load evaluation
- Machines States and Failures

Director can access the following:

- Personal vDisk data that allows for runtime monitoring showing base allocation and gives the IT helpdesk the ability to reset the Personal vDisk.
- Historical data stored in the Monitor database to access the Configuration Logging database.
- Real-time data from the Broker Agent using a unified console integrated with EdgeSight features, Performance Manager, and Network Inspector.
- ICA data from the NetScaler Gateway using HDX Insight.

Citrix Director uses a troubleshooting dashboard that provides real-time health monitoring of the XenApp or XenDesktop site. Using this dashboard, helpdesk personnel can resolve the entry-level support calls. This feature allows administrators to see disasters in real time, providing a better idea of what the end user is experiencing.

The following screenshot illustrates the statistical view from Citrix Director:

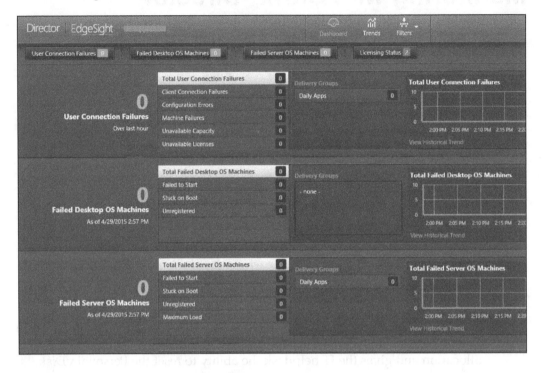

Session Recording on Citrix® Director

Session Recording records the on-screen activities of any user's session, from any server running the XenApp subject to corporate policy and regulatory compliance over any type of connection. Session Recording records, catalogs, and archives sessions for retrieval and playback.

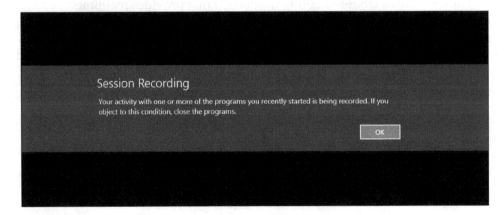

The following is the **Session Recording Authorization Console** screen, where we define the authentication policies for helpdesk engineers and administrators:

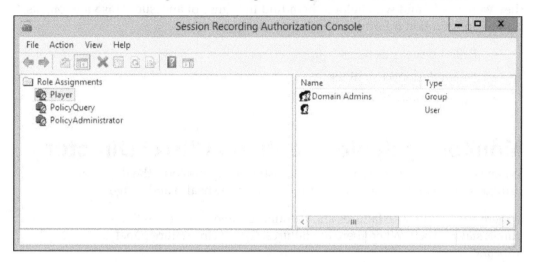

The Session Recording feature uses policies that start the recordings of application sessions automatically.

This enables administrators to monitor and inspect the user activity of applications, such as healthcare patient information systems and financial operations, security monitoring, and supporting internal controls for regulatory compliance. Similarly, Session Recording also helps in technical support by rapid problem identification and quick resolution.

Configuration logging on Citrix® Director

Configuration logging is a feature that allows Citrix administrators to keep a track of administrative changes to a XenDesktop or XenApp Site. This feature can help administrators analyze and troubleshoot problems after configuration changes are made, help in change management and track configurations, and report administration activity.

Using configuration logging, administrators can view in Director with the Trend View interface to provide notifications of configuration changes to administrators who do not have access to XenDesktop Citrix Studio.

The Trends View feature gives historical data of configuration changes over a period of time so administrators can measure what changes were made to the sites when they were made, and who helped them find the cause of an issue. This view breaks down configuration information into three categories:

- Failed server machines
- Failed desktop machines
- Connection failures

Monitoring deployments on Citrix® Director

When you open Director with full administrator permissions, the dashboard provides a consolidated location for monitoring the health and usage of a site.

If there are currently no failures and no failures have occurred in the past 60 minutes, panels stay warped. When there are failures, the specific failure panel automatically appears:

Panel	Description
Sessions Connected	Connected sessions across all delivery groups for the last 60 minutes.
User Connection Failures	Connection failures over the last 60 minutes. Click on the categories next to the total number to view metrics for that type of failure. In the adjacent table, that number is broken out by delivery groups.
Licensing Status	License Server alerts are sent by the License Server and also display the actions required to resolve the alert. Delivery controller alerts display the details of the licensing state as seen by the controller and are sent by the delivery controller.
Failed Desktop OS Machines or Failed Server OS Machines	Total failures in the last 60 minutes are broken out by delivery groups. Failures broken out by types include failed to start, stuck on boot, and unregistered. For server OS machines, failures also include machines reaching maximum load.
Infrastructure	This includes the health status of your site's hosts, controllers, and infrastructure. View performance alerts. For hosts, the connection status and the health of the CPU, memory, bandwidth (network usage), and storage (disk usage) are monitored using information from XenServer or VMware.
Average Logon Duration	This is the login data for the last 60 minutes. The large number on the left is the average login duration across the hour. Login data for VDAs earlier than XenDesktop 7.0 is not included in this average.

Monitoring sessions on Citrix® Director

If a session becomes disconnected, it is still active and its applications continue to run, but the user device is no longer communicating with the server.

If the user device is running a legacy **Virtual Delivery Agents (VDA)**, such as a VDA earlier than version 7, Director cannot display complete information about the session. Instead, it displays a message that the information is not available in the **User Details** view and **Activity Manager** panel:

Action	Description
View data over a longer period of time	In the Trends view, select the Sessions tab to drill down to more specific usage data for connected and disconnected sessions over a longer period of time (session totals from earlier than the last 60 minutes). To view this information, click on View historical trends.
View the total number of connected sessions across all Delivery Groups	From the Dashboard, in the Sessions Connected pane, view the total number of connected sessions across all Delivery Groups for the last 60 minutes. Then, click on the large total number, which opens the Filters view, where you can display graphical session data based on selected Delivery Groups and ranges and usage across Delivery Groups.
View a user's currently connected machine or session	From the Activity Manager and User Details views, view the user's currently connected machine or session and a list of all machines and sessions to which this user has access. To access this list, click on the session switcher icon in the user title bar.

Monitoring Hotfixes on Citrix® Director

To view the Hotfixes installed on a specific machine VDA (physical or VM), choose the **Machine Details** view.

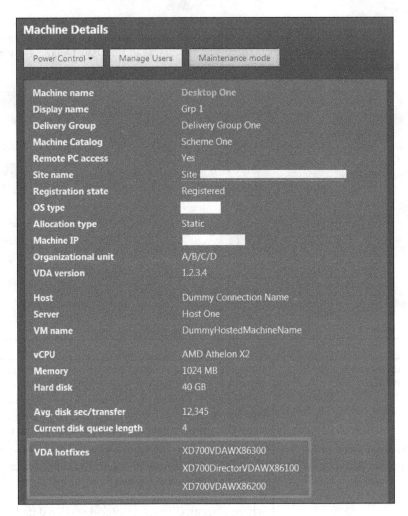

Controlling user machine power states

You can control the state of the machines that you select in Director, use the **Power Control** options. These options are available for Desktop OS machines, but might not be available for Server OS machines.

 This functionality is not available for physical machines or machines using remote PC access.

Command	Function
Start	This starts a VM when it is off (also called a cold start).
Restart	This performs a soft shutdown of the VM and all running processes are stopped individually before restarting the VM. For example, select machines that appear in Director as "failed to start," and use this command to restart them.
Resume	This command resumes a suspended VM and restores it in its previous running state.
Force Restart	This command restarts the VM without first performing a shutdown procedure. This command works in the same way as unplugging a physical server and then plugging it back in and turning it back on.
Shut Down	It performs a soft shutdown of the VM; all running processes are halted individually.
Suspend	This command suspends a running VM in its current state and stores that state in a file on the default storage repository. This option allows you to shut down the VM's host server and later, after rebooting it, resume the VM, returning it to its original running state.
Force Shutdown	This shuts down the VM without first performing a shutdown procedure the same way as unplugging a physical server. This might shut down all running processes and you will be at a risk of losing data.

NetScaler Insight Center™ for monitoring XenApp®

In the cloud, mobile, and virtual desktop environments, applications are deployed in a dynamic and circulated manner. In such an environment, monitoring and diagnosing the application issues can be a challenge for IT administrators, which can affect the end-user experience and overall employee productivity.

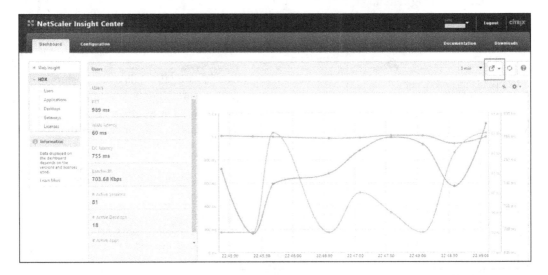

NetScaler Insight Center is a virtual appliance that runs on Microsoft Hyper-V, VMWare ESX, and XenServer addresses the application perceptibility challenge by collecting detailed information about virtual desktop traffic and web applications, such as flow, web page performance data, user-session-level information, and database information flowing through the NetScaler Gateway appliances, NetScaler ADCs or CloudBridge appliances at your site and providing actionable reports. NetScaler Insight Center helps IT administrators to troubleshoot and proactively monitor customer issues in a short time.

NetScaler Insight Center provides insight into all of the components that might affect application performance and helps you analyze the performance of the applications running on your appliances.

NetScaler Insight Center™ components

The following are the components of NetScaler Insight Center:

- NetScaler Web Insight provides data analytics for web traffic flowing through NetScaler ADCs.

- HDX Insight provides data analytics for XenApp and XenDesktop traffic flowing through NetScaler ADCs, NetScaler Gateway appliances, or CloudBridge appliances. HDX Insight collects reports when NetScaler ADCs are configured in transparent mode, and when NetScaler Gateway appliances are configured in single-hop mode or double-hop mode.

- NetScaler WAN Insight provides data analytics for both augmented and unaugmented traffic flowing through CloudBridge appliances.

NetScaler Web Insight

NetScaler Web Insight delivers visibility into web applications and allows Citrix administrators to monitor all web applications being served by NetScaler ADCs. Web Insight captures data of web traffic that flows between the clients and the servers. It also generates AppFlow records by inspecting the data and presents the records in visual formats. These reports deliver critical information, such as user and server response time, allowing Citrix administrators to improve web application performance.

 NetScaler Insight Center was earlier called NetScaler Insight. At the time of rebranding, the release number was changed from 1.0 to 10.1, aligning with a NetScaler release.

Key features of NetScaler Web Insight include URL specific reports, application-specific reports, and cache server-specific reports that provide visibility into cache performance. Web Insight also provides reflectivity into HTTP response status, HTTP request methods, user agents, and client operating systems.

Information received from Web Insight about client-side parameters enables administrators to evaluate end user experience. Along with other competencies, you can identify the top web applications accessed by clients and track their ultimate usage.

Citrix administrators can use Web Insight to answer any of the following questions:

- What operating system and browser is a particular client using?
- While accessing a particular application such as ShareFile, which clients are experiencing high latency?
- In the past hour, which applications have had the most hits?
- Which applications or servers are sending the most error-related responses?
- For any given client, what are the applications and URLs that have been accessed?

NetScaler HDX Insight™

NetScaler HDX Insight delivers Citrix administrators an easy way to monitor users and the performance of the applications hosted on NetScaler Gateway, NetScaler ADCs, and CloudBridge appliances. NetScaler HDX Insight captures the ICA traffic data that flows between the clients and the servers, generates AppFlow records by inspection of the data, and presents the records as visual reports.

HDX is built on top of the Citrix ICA protocol. ICA is a Citrix proprietary protocol used in XenApp/XenDesktop traffic. It is composed of virtual channels. A virtual channel is a connection used for the interchange of comprehensive packet data between a Citrix XenApp or XenDesktop and the Citrix Receiver online plug-in. Connections for graphics, sound, printing, end user experience monitoring, and client drive mapping are a few examples of the virtual channels.

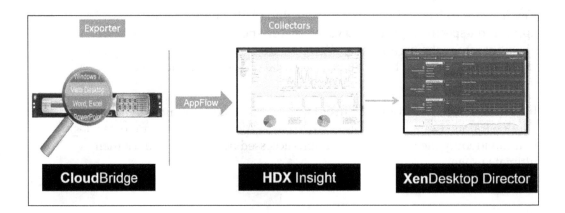

With NetScaler HDX Insight, Citrix administrators can troubleshoot issues while accessing a particular published application through XenApp or XenDesktop. For example, the administrators of Citrix XenApp and Citrix XenDesktop environments can use HDX Insight to answer the following questions:

- Which XenApp or XenDesktop users are consuming the most bandwidth over a given time period?

- Which part of the network, the first **Demilitarized zone (DMZ)** or the second DMZ, is causing a bad user experience?

- For a given XenDesktop user, what is the average client and server-side latency, and the average jitter?

- What are the top applications across all XenApp users, by the up-time and the total number of launches over a given time period?

- Which virtual channels are consuming the most bandwidth over a given time period?

- What is the DC latency at the datacenter end of the CloudBridge appliance?

NetScaler Insight Center also collects information from the CloudBridge datacenter and branch appliances.

 NetScaler Insight Center can also be integrated with Desktop Director. In this case, to enable HDX Insight data collection, you must configure the NetScaler Insight Center virtual appliance in Desktop Director.

NetScaler WAN Insight

A Citrix CloudBridge delivers a large number of applications by greatly improving the efficiency of data flow across the network. Improving productivity requires monitoring your network. For example, the poor performance of any critical applications can increase the delay in application delivery, and a particular branch office using maximum bandwidth can cause delays at other branch offices.

The Citrix WAN Insight feature of NetScaler Insight Center gives CloudBridge administrators an easy way to monitor the accelerated and unaccelerated WAN traffic that flows through datacenter and branch appliances, and it provides end-to-end visibility, such as application-specific data, client-specific data, and branch- specific data. With the ability to identify and monitor all the applications, clients, and branches on the network, you can efficiently deal with the issues that reduce the performance.

This feature also provides powerful capabilities for failure analysis of your applications, network, and branches. Live and historical reports enable you to be aware of performance issues before users raise complaints.

As a CloudBridge administrator, you can use WAN Insight to answer questions such as:

- Which client in a branch office is consuming the most bandwidth?
- What is the latency at the CloudBridge datacenter appliance?
- What compression ratio is achieved at a particular branch?

Optimizing Citrix XenApp®

Citrix XenApp and XenDesktop are both solutions that deliver apps and desktops as an on-demand service. Basically, Citrix XenApp and XenDesktop depend on the Citrix ICA protocol, which imparts collaborative screen information and the data of other applications between desktops running in a centralized datacenter and the remote user's end devices. ICA is a highly effective protocol that delivers the best performance for single user access over a high latency and low bandwidth network.

In our previous topics, we have already seen how Citrix CloudBridge or WanScaler optimize the end-to-end ICA connection. CloudBridge plays a tremendous part in XenDesktop deployments, where the demands of increasing users are high at the same bandwidth consumption. CloudBridge entirely supports all levels of ICA encryption to keep an end-to-end security at the required standard while optimizing traffic delivered to other branches.

We can dive deep into Citrix CloudBridge with the following link: `https://www.citrix.com/products/cloudbridge/overview.html`.

There are many optimization guides already available on Citrix XenApp, that we should definitely go through before planning our new XenApp deployment:

- *Windows 2008 R2 Optimization Guide For Desktop Virtualization with XenApp 6/6.5* (`http://support.citrix.com/servlet/KbServlet/download/29413-102-664317/`)
- *How to Optimize XenDesktop Machines* (`http://support.citrix.com/article/CTX125874`)

Summary

In this chapter, we saw how to monitor Citrix XenApp using Citrix Director and EdgeSight, and how to optimize the Citrix XenApp infrastructure using various toolkits, such as Citrix NetScaler Insight Center, Citrix NetScaler HDX Insight, Citrix NetScaler WAN Insight, and Citrix NetScaler Web Insight. At the end of this topic, we saw some optimization tips and guides that we can try in our XenApp environment to optimize our infrastructure and improve the productivity in end user computing.

Index

Thank you for buying
Troubleshooting Citrix XenApp®

About Packt Publishing

Packt, pronounced 'packed', published its first book, *Mastering phpMyAdmin for Effective MySQL Management*, in April 2004, and subsequently continued to specialize in publishing highly focused books on specific technologies and solutions.

Our books and publications share the experiences of your fellow IT professionals in adapting and customizing today's systems, applications, and frameworks. Our solution-based books give you the knowledge and power to customize the software and technologies you're using to get the job done. Packt books are more specific and less general than the IT books you have seen in the past. Our unique business model allows us to bring you more focused information, giving you more of what you need to know, and less of what you don't.

Packt is a modern yet unique publishing company that focuses on producing quality, cutting-edge books for communities of developers, administrators, and newbies alike. For more information, please visit our website at www.packtpub.com.

About Packt Enterprise

In 2010, Packt launched two new brands, Packt Enterprise and Packt Open Source, in order to continue its focus on specialization. This book is part of the Packt Enterprise brand, home to books published on enterprise software – software created by major vendors, including (but not limited to) IBM, Microsoft, and Oracle, often for use in other corporations. Its titles will offer information relevant to a range of users of this software, including administrators, developers, architects, and end users.

Writing for Packt

We welcome all inquiries from people who are interested in authoring. Book proposals should be sent to author@packtpub.com. If your book idea is still at an early stage and you would like to discuss it first before writing a formal book proposal, then please contact us; one of our commissioning editors will get in touch with you.

We're not just looking for published authors; if you have strong technical skills but no writing experience, our experienced editors can help you develop a writing career, or simply get some additional reward for your expertise.

Citrix® XenDesktop® 7 Cookbook

ISBN: 978-1-78217-746-3   Paperback: 410 pages

Over 35 recipes to help you implement a fully featured XenDesktop® 7 architecture with a rich and powerful VDI experience

1. Implement the XenDesktop 7 architecture and its satellite components.

2. Learn how to publish desktops and applications to the end-user devices, optimizing their performance and increasing the general security.

3. Designed in a manner which will allow you to progress gradually from one chapter to another or to implement a single component only referring to the specific topic.

Getting Started with Citrix XenApp 6.5

ISBN: 978-1-84968-666-2   Paperback: 478 pages

Design and implement Citrix farms based on XenApp 6.5

1. Use Citrix management tools to publish applications and resources on client devices with this book and eBook.

2. Deploy and optimize XenApp 6.5 on Citrix XenServer, VMware ESX, and Microsoft Hyper-V virtual machines and physical servers.

3. Understand new features included in XenApp 6.5 including a brand new chapter on advanced XenApp deployment covering topics such as unattended install of XenApp 6.5, using dynamic data center provisioning, and more.

Please check **www.PacktPub.com** for information on our titles

Mastering Citrix® XenServer®

ISBN: 978-1-78328-739-0   Paperback: 300 pages

Design and implement highly optimized virtualization solutions using Citrix® XenServer® 6.2

1. Master mission-critical aspects of virtualization to develop, deploy, and administer virtual infrastructures.

2. Integrate Citrix XenServer with OpenStack and CloudStack to create a private cloud.

3. Implement automation with command-line Windows PowerShell scripting.

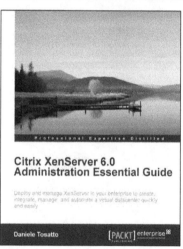

Citrix XenServer 6.0 Administration Essential Guide

ISBN: 978-1-84968-616-7   Paperback: 364 pages

Deploy and manage XenServer in your enterprise to create, integrate, manage and automate a virtual datacenter quickly and easily

1. This book and eBook will take you through deploying XenServer in your enterprise, and teach you how to create and maintain your datacenter.

2. Manage XenServer and virtual machines using Citrix management tools and the command line.

3. Organize secure access to your infrastructure using role-based access control.

Please check **www.PacktPub.com** for information on our titles